EAT BEAUTIFUL

Secrets From a Bone Broth Kitchen

Soups and Stews for Your Wellness Diet

80 Paleo, AIP, GAPS, GAPS Intro, Keto and VAD Recipes

A COOKBOOK BY
MEGAN STEVENS

Find recipes and insights at my blog, EAT BEAUTIFUL *(www.eatbeautiful.net), and Pinterest account (https://www. pinterest.com/ eatbeautifulnet/).*

TABLE OF CONTENTS

CHAPTER THREE: Dairy-Free Soups and Stews
[with nightshades, seeds or legumes]

CHAPTER FOUR: *Soups and Stews With Dairy*

CHAPTER FIVE: *Soup-Making Secrets*

APPENDIX: SOUP STAPLES RECIPES

Broths and Stocks

BASIC COOKED VEGETABLES FOR USE IN SOUPS

BASIC MEATBALLS FOR USE IN SOUPS

OTHER BASICS FOR USE IN SOUPS

RESOURCE GUIDE

INDEX

SPECIAL THANKS |

gentle soups

CHAPTER ONE

Gentle Soups

"Gentle" means different things to different people. While many remedial
diets share healing concepts, contradictions exist, as well —
or different bodies might require different approaches.
Basically speaking, all of the soups in this chapter qualify as gentle —
even *extra*-gentle — for most people.
Most of the recipes in this chapter serve the following diets:
Paleo, GAPS, GAPS Introduction Diet, AIP and VAD.
There are several Keto recipes in this chapter, as well.
One precept you'll see in these gentle soups
is that most of them are simmered or slow cooked,
as opposed to broiled, grilled, roasted or sautéed.
The ingredients are also unlikely to cause inflammation.

Basic Chicken Meatballs Soup

Paleo, GAPS, GAPS Intro, AIP+, Keto+, VAD+

A clear buttery broth, comfortable carrots, creamy celeriac cubes and fresh herbs with light chicken meatballs make a wonderful, gentle soup. (The secret to light meatballs is using a combination of apple cider vinegar and baking soda, which react and create a rise within the meatballs. While baking soda isn't used on the GAPS Intro diet, in this case it is acceptable because it is neutralized by the apple cider vinegar — it won't make the belly pH alkaline.)

Serves 4 to 6.

INGREDIENTS:

1-1/2 pounds ground chicken thighs

6 cups bone broth or meat stock

6 carrots, peeled and chopped (use fennel for Keto, use white carrots or turnips for VAD)

1 large celeriac (also called celery root), peeled and cubed

1/4 cup water

4 cloves garlic, crushed or minced

1 tablespoon apple cider vinegar (or use lemon juice)

1-1/2 teaspoons sea salt

1/2 teaspoon baking soda

1/4 teaspoon white or black pepper (omit for AIP)

Fresh herbs of choice: dill, Italian parsley, basil, chopped (use fresh rosemary or sage for VAD)

INSTRUCTIONS:

1. Place ground chicken in large mixing bowl. Add water, apple cider vinegar, sea salt, baking soda and pepper. Stir together well.

2. Heat bone broth over high heat in large saucepan or stock pot. While broth heats, form ground meat mixture into meatballs of desired size.

3. When broth comes to a boil, add meatballs, carrots (or fennel or turnips), celeriac and garlic. Lower heat so the broth simmers slowly. Simmer until chicken meatballs are cooked through and veggies are tender, about 20 to 25 minutes.

4. Serve soup topped with fresh herbs.

Bone Marrow Soup

Paleo, GAPS, GAPS Intro, AIP, VAD

The best way to make bone marrow soup is to first make meat stock with marrow bones, water and sea salt. I like to top my soup with a poached egg (not for the elimination stage of AIP) because poached eggs and whole pieces of marrow are delicious together. The marrow may also be puréed into the soup base (as described below) if you don't enjoy eating it separately. I photographed this soup on the thicker side so the marrow and slow-cooked beef could be seen, but more meat stock can be added for a thinner, yet still creamy, base. I also excluded the egg from the photo, but you can imagine the variations: creamy high-fat veggie meat stock purée, slow-cooked beef, marrow and optional poached eggs. This soup is very rich, even more so when extra meat stock is added. It's a great soup for GAPS Intro, but also a gentle soup for most wellness protocols. I designate winter squash to be used for GAPS and a trio of root vegetables to be used in the base for VAD. Paleo and AIP can choose between the two options.

Serves 4 to 6, depending on the amount of stock and meat used.

INGREDIENTS:

10 cups water

3 to 5 pounds marrow bones (or marrow bones attached to beef shank)

2 to 3 pounds chuck roast (optional), if no beef shank (meat) comes with the marrow bones

1 pound parsnips + 1 turnip + 1 celery root (VAD), or 1 butternut squash (GAPS and GAPS Intro)

2 large onions, peeled and roughly chopped

3 tablespoons avocado oil (only 1 tablespoon needed for GAPS version), or butter or ghee for VAD, if preferred

2 tablespoons sea salt + 1-1/2 teaspoons (or + 1/2 teaspoon for GAPS), divided use

2 teaspoons dried rosemary (for VAD) or other dried herb of choice (such as basil or parsley)

INSTRUCTIONS:

1. Make meat stock (see Recipe Notes).

2. While stock cooks, preheat oven to 350 degrees Fahrenheit. Line a cookie sheet or casserole dish with parchment paper.

3. If on GAPS or using butternut squash, poke a hole into center of winter squash, to allow steam to escape. Place winter squash to one side of parchment paper.

4. Bake squash 30 minutes, then remove from oven. Place onions to other side of cookie sheet. Add avocado oil (or melted butter) and 1/2 teaspoon sea salt to the onions. Toss to coat.

5. Bake winter squash and onions until knife inserts into center easily. Cooking times will vary based on squash size, about 30 to 45 minutes more. If onions are getting too brown, remove them to a dish while winter squash finishes baking.

6. If on VAD or using parsnip veggie combination, peel and roughly chop all three kinds of root vegetables.

7. Place parsnip-root veggie combination and onions on large cookie sheet. Add avocado oil (or melted butter) and 1-1/2 teaspoons sea salt. Toss to coat.

8. Bake root vegetables about 45 minutes, until softened but not too brown. (Watch parsnips closely, as they are apt to burn. Turn heat down to 325 degrees Fahrenheit and flip parsnips over if they are browning too quickly.)

9. When stock is finished cooking, use a handheld colander spoon to remove bones, marrow and meat solids from stock. Set aside to cool.

10. When cool, jolt the marrow from each bone by thumping it hard on the counter. (Some of the marrow may fall out into the stock on its own.) In most cases, the marrow will easily fall out. Use cracked crab tools or a small spoon or knife to scoop out any marrow that doesn't come out easily.

11. If using winter squash, scoop about 4 cups squash flesh from peel. Place in blender. Add onions, dried herbs of choice and about 4 cups warm meat stock. Purée marrow into stock with winter squash or leave marrow separate in large chunks, whichever you prefer.

12. If using parsnip veggie combination, place roasted veggies and 4 cups stock into blender. Add marrow or keep separate. Add dried herb of choice. Purée about 30 seconds until mostly smooth.

13. Pour veggie-stock purée into large saucepan. After removing large chunks of fat from beef shank meat or chuck roast, add chunks of meat to soup. Add extra meat stock to create desired soup thickness. (Reserve remaining meat stock for another use.) Heat.

14. Serve soup and any slow-cooked beef from the bone with optional marrow (if kept separate) and optional poached eggs on top (not AIP).

RECIPE NOTES:

See Meat Stock recipe on Page 136.

See How to Soft-Boil Eggs on Page 153.

See How to Poach or Fry Eggs on Page 154.

Beet Soup With Eggs or Steaks

Paleo, GAPS, GAPS Intro

This soup can be served chilled with hard-boiled eggs, or hot with eggs or steak. For GAPS Intro, it's a nice change either way. If you use the steak option, whole steaks are poached in the soup, removed to slice and placed back in the hot soup. This cooking method makes them gentle for GAPS Intro, but also cooks the steaks nicely, allowing for gentle, medium-rare (or more well-done, if preferred) cooking. This soup can be quite beautiful and gourmet, despite the humble diet it serves. This soup can also be quite inexpensive if prepared with eggs or wild game. The first time I made it, I used wild elk steaks. A very affordable and convenient dinner with hard or soft-boiled eggs.

Serves 4.

INGREDIENTS:

3 cups bone broth

1 pound beets, peeled and diced

1 large yellow onion, peeled and diced

1 cup yogurt or kefir, (fully cultured for 24 hours for GAPS), optional

2 cloves garlic, minced or crushed

1 teaspoon dried dill

1/2 teaspoon sea salt

Optional: 1-pound steaks (see Variation)

Garnishes: hard-, medium- or soft-boiled eggs; green onions; fresh dill; sour cream

INSTRUCTIONS:

1. Place broth, beets, onions, dill and sea salt in a medium pot. Bring to a boil.

2. Turn heat down to low or medium-low. Cover and simmer until beets and onions are tender, about 25 minutes. (See Recipe Notes if cooking steaks in your soup.)

3. Stir in garlic. If serving cold, chill a minimum of 3 hours.

4. When ready to serve hot or cold, ladle soup into bowls. Garnish and serve.

VARIATION:

1. If you're cooking steaks in your soup, add them to the simmering beets and broth after the first 15 minutes of cooking have elapsed (set a timer). Poach the steaks in slow simmering broth for up to 10 minutes, longer if you want your steaks well done.

2. Remove one to a cutting board and cut deeply into the middle to see how done it is.

3. Once steaks are cooked to your liking, use tongs to remove them to a cutting board. Slice each steak into thin strips. Or cut into small bite-size cubes, if preferred.

4. After ladling soup into each bowl, top each serving with fanned slices of steak. Or stir cubes of steak into soup before serving.

5. Garnish with optional hard-boiled eggs, green onions, fresh dill, sour cream and other toppings.

RECIPE NOTES:

See How to Soft-Boil Eggs on Page 153.

You can really "go pretty" with this soup if you're feeling like more fresh produce: Additionally, you can garnish with peeled and diced cucumbers, avocado and edible flowers.

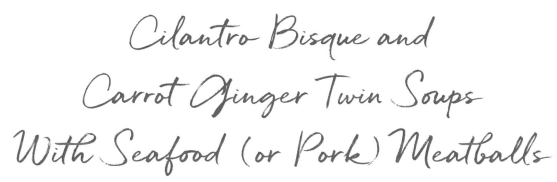

Cilantro Bisque and Carrot Ginger Twin Soups With Seafood (or Pork) Meatballs

Paleo, GAPS, GAPS Intro, AIP

Usually, a GAPS Intro soup will only have simmered meats and vegetables, because the goal is to consume only soft textures. This soup gives the option of simmered onions or roasted onions, because the roasted onions are then puréed, rendering them smooth and gentle. This soup is low-lectin.

Serves 4 to 6.

INGREDIENTS:

6 cups meat stock, warmed

4 onions, peeled and chopped roughly

1 to 2 pounds seafood (or pork) meatballs (see Recipe Notes)

1 pound fennel bulb, diced (or peeled zucchini, if preferred)

1 pound carrots, sliced

1 bunch green onions, chopped, whites and greens separated

1 bunch fresh cilantro, stems included, washed well, reserving some for garnish

1/4 cup fat of choice, divided use (ghee, butter, lard etc; use a dairy-free fat for AIP)

3-inch piece fresh ginger

4 cloves fresh garlic, minced or crushed

2 teaspoons sea salt

INSTRUCTIONS:

1. Preheat oven to 375 degrees Fahrenheit.

2. Place 2 tablespoons fat of choice in large casserole dish or roasting pan. Add onions and sea salt, and toss to coat. Bake onions 40 minutes, until slightly browned and tender. Remove from oven, and allow to cool partially.

3. While onions bake, bring 3 cups meat stock to a simmer in large saucepan. Add fennel, carrots and whites of green onions. Cover and simmer over medium heat 15 minutes.

4. Allow simmered fennel-carrot mixture to cool slightly, then pour into blender and purée until smooth.

5. Pour fennel-carrot purée into saucepan and heat over medium heat.

6. Place onions in blender with 3 cups stock. Add green parts of green onions, fresh cilantro, remaining 2 tablespoons fat, fresh ginger and fresh garlic. Purée on medium speed 30 to 50 seconds, until smooth.

7. Add meatballs to slow-simmering fennel-carrot purée in pot. Poach about 10 minutes, until fully cooked.

8. Use a second saucepan to heat the cilantro bisque over medium heat. Do not allow to simmer.

9. Serve carrot meatball soup first. Then pour in cilantro soup to one side of each bowl.

RECIPE NOTES

See Ground Meat and Herb Meatballs on Page 150.

15-Minute Beef Stew With Skirt Steak

Paleo, GAPS+, AIP+, Keto, VAD

Beef stew in 15 minutes is possible because of skirt steak. This recipe really does cook up in 15 minutes, not including chopping the veggies and slicing the meat. This timeframe is possible because we make a stir-fry and then a quick gravy. The result is very stew-like, but I love that it's one of the fastest dinners I can make for our family. If you haven't worked with skirt steak before, I found it only a few years ago myself when a butcher told me it was an economical option for stir-fries. My boys love steak, so this cut allows me to buy it more often. I love stew and gravy, so this preparation wins for all of us.

Serves 4 to 5.

INGREDIENTS:

1-1/2 pounds skirt steak

1 to 2 onions sliced

1 fennel bulb, sliced

1/2 pound radishes, sliced

6 ounces shiitake mushrooms, whole or sliced, according to preference

1 cup bone broth or meat stock

2 tablespoons sesame oil (sub avocado oil for AIP)

1 tablespoon tapioca flour (not GAPS)

1 tablespoon garlic powder

1 teaspoon ginger powder

1-1/2 teaspoons sea salt, divided use

INSTRUCTIONS:

1. Slice steak according to directions (see Recipe Notes). Set aside.

2. Heat wok or large skillet over medium-high heat. Add sesame oil, onions, fennel, radishes, mushrooms and 1/2 teaspoon sea salt.

3. Sauté 8 to 10 minutes, stirring often.

4. Add beef, garlic, ginger and remaining sea salt. Sauté, stirring and turning meat over constantly, 3 to 5 minutes. (Do not overcook, or skirt steak will be chewy.)

5. In a small bowl, stir together broth and tapioca until well-mixed. (Skip this step for GAPS.)

6. Add broth to pan and stir well until sauce has thickened, 1 to 2 minutes.

7. Serve.

RECIPE NOTES:

Skirt steak comes rolled up like a spool of ribbon or a cinnamon roll. To prepare skirt steak for optimum tenderness, cut the roll in half. Flop one half to its flat side on a cutting board. Slice thinly, creating rainbow shapes. (Thus, the meat is cut against its grain, rendering it more tender.) Repeat with the second half of the roll and any remaining steak until all of the meat is thinly sliced.

Fall and Winter Meatball Soup

Paleo, GAPS, GAPS Intro, AIP+, VAD+

Serves 8.

INGREDIENTS:

6 cups bone broth

1 large butternut or kabocha winter squash, baked in its skin (see Recipe Notes); (for VAD, use 4 large, hot potatoes, fresh from the boiling water)

2 pounds full fat ground beef, lamb, buffalo or turkey thigh

1 bunch fresh spinach, approximately 8 ounces (not VAD)

1 tablespoon dried basil (use dried sage for VAD)

1-1/2 teaspoons sea salt

1 teaspoon white pepper (not AIP)

INSTRUCTIONS:

1. Place 3 cups broth in large saucepan. Heat to a simmer over medium-high heat.

2. Make beef meatballs in large bowl, combining raw meat with dried basil (or sage for VAD), sea salt and white pepper (omit for AIP).

3. Add meatballs to simmering broth. Simmer 15 to 20 minutes, until meatballs are cooked through. Add spinach for the last 5 minutes of cooking.

4. While meatballs cook, add remaining 3 cups broth to blender with 3 cups winter squash (or the equivalent of 2 potatoes for VAD).

5. When the meatballs are cooked, add desired amount of remaining flesh from baked winter squash to pot. (For VAD, add potatoes in place of winter squash.)

6. Add purée from blender to pot with meatballs. The base can be as brothy or thick and bisque-like as you prefer. I find the bisque-like base is usually more satisfying and preferred. But sometimes, especially for an invalid, the broth base is preferable.

7. Heat the soup to hot, and serve.

RECIPE NOTES:

See How to Bake Winter Squash on Page 149.

Simple Fennel and Cauliflower Rice Soup With Shredded Chicken

(with Instant Pot version)
Paleo, GAPS, GAPS Intro, AIP+, Keto, VAD+

Serves 5 to 6.

INGREDIENTS:

6 cups water

2 pounds boneless, skinless chicken thighs

2 bulbs fennel, diced

24 ounces fresh cauliflower, riced, or frozen cauliflower rice (or use 1 diced cabbage for VAD)

1/4 cup butter or ghee (use coconut oil for AIP)

2 teaspoons sea salt

freshly ground black pepper to taste (not AIP)

INSTRUCTIONS:

1. Place into stock pot: water, fennel, chicken and sea salt. Bring to a simmer over high heat. Reduce heat, cover and simmer slowly 25 to 30 minutes, until fennel is soft and chicken is cooked through.

2. Use a slotted spoon to remove chicken pieces to a large plate or cutting board.

3. Add cauliflower rice to the stock pot. Turn up heat to medium-high. When the stock returns to a simmer, reduce heat slightly and cook 5 minutes.

4. While cauliflower cooks, cut chicken into bite-size pieces. Return chicken to the pot.

5. Serve topped with fresh fennel fronds (not VAD) and generous pats of butter or ghee (if desired and if dairy is tolerated).

INSTANT POT INSTRUCTIONS:

1. Place into Instant Pot: water, fennel, chicken and sea salt. Seal lid and shut steam valve. Press "Soup" setting, and reduce time to 15 minutes using "-" button.

2. When timer goes off, press "Cancel" button. Allow pressure to release naturally for 1 hour. Carefully open steam vent. Remove lid.

3. Use a slotted spoon to remove chicken pieces to a large plate or cutting board.

4. Add frozen cauliflower rice to Instant Pot. Press "Sauté" button. Cover with glass lid. When soup begins to simmer, allow cauliflower to cook 5 minutes.

5. Press "Cancel" button.

6. While cauliflower cooks, cut chicken into bite-size pieces. Return chicken to the pot.

7. Serve topped with fresh fennel fronds (not VAD) and generous pats of butter or ghee (if desired and if dairy is tolerated).

Hamburger Soup

Paleo, GAPS, GAPS Intro, AIP+, Keto, VAD+

This recipe is for those of us who want a hamburger while on the GAPS Intro Diet, the VAD diet (omit avocado) or the first elimination stage of the AIP diet. It's soup, for sure. But it's a fun variation on hamburgers for dinner. The meat patties poach in the rich meat stock instead of the usual preparations for burgers, in accordance with GAPS principles for gentle textures and cooking methods.

Serves 4 to 6.

INGREDIENTS:

1 to 2 pounds ground beef, bison or lamb, depending on how many you're serving and whether you want leftovers

4 cups meat stock

1 to 2 avocados, sliced thinly

2 onions, sliced thinly

1/2 cup sauerkraut

4 cloves garlic, optional

1 teaspoon (or less, to taste) sea salt

freshly ground pepper to taste (not AIP)

INSTRUCTIONS:

1. Form ground beef into 4 to 6 equal-size patties.

2. In a large, deep frying pan, bring stock to a simmer. Add onions and simmer over medium heat, covered, 5 minutes. Open lid, stir onions and cook 5 minutes more.

3. Add garlic to the onions and stir slightly. Place patties on top of onions. Sprinkle with sea salt and optional black pepper. Replace lid and simmer 5 minutes more.

4. Remove lid and flip burgers. Assess cooking time based on how you like your burgers cooked. Keep in mind that good grass-fed beef is healthiest when served rare or medium-rare. Cook burgers on second side about 2 minutes, or to desired doneness (see Recipe Notes).

5. Use broad, shallow bowls, if you have them, to serve burgers. Ladle onions and broth into each dish. Top with burgers and more onions. Top burgers with fanned slices of avocado and a heaping pile of sauerkraut (or less if you haven't worked up to larger amounts of probiotics yet).

RECIPE NOTES:

To check for doneness, use the finger test: When you press a finger into the center of a patty, there should be some "give"; the meat should not be firm or hard. Stop cooking the meat when it has the give of the soft spot of your palm just below your thumb.

Chicken Zoodle Soup

(with Instant Pot version)
Paleo, GAPS, GAPS Intro, AIP, Keto+, VAD+
{A "Dump and Cook" Recipe}

This recipe is another of the "Dump and Cook" recipes that still manages to turn out a rich, buttery broth and satisfying "noodles." The Keto and VAD versions omit the carrots.

Serves 4 to 6.

INGREDIENTS:

6 cups water

2 pounds zucchini, peeled and spiralized (see Recipe Notes)

1-1/2 pounds chicken thighs, boneless and skinless

3 carrots, chopped small (omit for Keto and use white carrots for VAD if you can find them)

3 celery stalks, chopped small

1 tablespoon sea salt

fresh dill, rosemary, parsley or thyme, chopped small (fresh rosemary or sage only for VAD)

Optional toppings: butter, or (not VAD) bacon fat or coconut oil

INSTRUCTIONS:

1. Place water, chicken thighs and sea salt in a medium-size saucepan. Bring to a boil, then reduce to a simmer. Cover and simmer chicken 30 minutes over low heat.

2. Use tongs or a slotted spoon to remove chicken thighs to a plate to cool slightly.

3. Add carrots and celery to slowly simmering broth. Simmer 5 minutes.

4. While broth and veggies cook, chop chicken into bite-size pieces.

5. Add zoodles to broth. Cook 2 to 3 minutes.

6. Turn off heat. Add chicken and fresh herbs.

7. Top with additional fat if desired, and serve.

INSTANT POT INSTRUCTIONS:

1. Place water, chicken thighs and sea salt into Instant Pot. Secure lid, make sure steam valve is shut, press "Soup" button and set for 30 minutes.

2. When timer goes off, allow pressure to release naturally for 1 hour, or do a quick release by pressing the "Cancel" button and carefully opening the steam valve.

3. Use tongs or a slotted spoon to remove chicken thighs to a plate to cool slightly.

4. Press "Sauté" button. Add carrots and celery to Instant Pot.

5. While broth heats, chop chicken into bite-size pieces.

6.When broth is about to simmer, add zoodles. Cook 2 to 3 minutes.

7. Press "Cancel" button. Add chicken and fresh herbs.

8. Top with additional fat if desired, and serve.

RECIPE NOTES:

See Resource Guide for a link to my favorite spiralizer, Page 161.

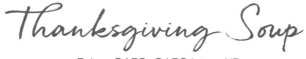
Thanksgiving Soup

Paleo, GAPS, GAPS Intro, AIP

The trick of this soup is keeping it gentle for the GAPS Intro Diet. We cook the ground meat directly in the broth, so it's not sautéed. The broth also helps the meat to easily break up into little pieces. The winter squash and onions, while baked, are cooked within their outer skins, which keeps the flesh that we use in the soup soft. The whole process just happens to also be easy and a bit fun, not to mention efficient and delicious. Who knew GAPS Intro could be such a pleasure? Of course, this soup is extra-special when winter squash is abundant.

Serves 6.

INGREDIENTS:

7 cups meat stock (see Recipe Notes)

1 large butternut or kabocha squash, baked whole (see Recipe Notes). Set aside about 1/3 of the cooked squash to purée, and cut the remaining squash into bite-size cubes.

2 large onions, or 4 small onions, baked whole (see Recipe Notes)

1 pound ground turkey (or other ground meat if preferred)

1 head cauliflower, chopped into bite-size pieces

1 small bunch collard greens, kale or spinach, washed well, ribs chopped and set aside separately and leaves chopped small

4 celery stalks, chopped (not GAPS Intro unless well-cooked)

2 large carrots, chopped

2 teaspoons dried thyme

1 teaspoon sea salt

1 teaspoon dried onion powder

1/2 teaspoon dried allspice (not AIP)

INSTRUCTIONS:

1. Heat 4 cups meat stock in a large saucepan over high heat. Add chopped cauliflower, carrots and celery. Simmer 15 minutes.

2. While veggies simmer, place remaining stock in a blender with winter squash flesh (just the flesh from around the seed cavity, or if kabocha, about 1/3 of the flesh) and peeled baked onions. Purée on medium-high speed for 30 seconds. Set aside.

3. To simmering meat stock in saucepan, add ground turkey, center ribs from leafy greens and sea salt. Break up meat consistently as the broth simmers. Cook 8 to 10 minutes, until meat is cooked through and in small pieces.

4. Add onion powder, thyme, allspice and leaves from leafy greens. Stir well.

5. Add purée from blender and winter squash cubes. Stir again.

6. Taste and serve.

RECIPE NOTES:

See Meat Stock recipe on Page 136.
See How and Why to Bake Onions on Page 146.
See How to Bake Winter Squash on Page 149.

Fresh Sole or Flounder With Celery Root and Artichokes

Paleo, GAPS, GAPS Intro, AIP, Keto+, VAD

Another gentle soup for GAPS Intro (and all the diets in this book), the fish and veggies cook in simmering broth.

Serves 4.

INGREDIENTS:

4 cups bone broth or meat stock

1 pound fresh sole or flounder fillets

2 onions, diced

1 head celery, diced

1 celery root, peeled and cut into 1/2-inch cubes

1 turnip, peeled and cut into 1/2-inch cubes

10 to 12 ounces frozen artichokes, defrosted for 1 hour and roughly chopped

2 tablespoons fat of choice

1-1/2 teaspoons sea salt

INSTRUCTIONS:

1. Heat large skillet or Dutch oven over medium-high heat. Add fat, onions, celery and sea salt. Cook 8 to 10 minutes, until slightly softened.

2. Add broth, celery root and turnips. Cover and simmer over medium-low heat about 15 minutes until veggies are cooked through.

3. Ladle 2 cups of broth and vegetables into a small bowl. Allow to cool for 10 to 15 minutes while fish simmers (next step).

4. Add artichoke hearts and fish fillets to remaining soup in pot. Simmer over medium-low heat, covered,

about 5 minutes, or up to 10 minutes for thicker fillets. (Do not overcook.) Fish is done when you can just begin to flake off big chunks with a spoon.

5. Place reserved broth and vegetables into blender. Pulse or purée to your liking, about 20 seconds. Add back to pot with fish.

6. Serve chunks of fish fillets with veggies and broth.

Find recipes and insights at my blog, EAT BEAUTIFUL *(www.eatbeautiful.net), and Pinterest account (https://www. pinterest.com/ eatbeautifulnet/).*

Turkey Sage Soup

(with Instant Pot version)
Paleo, GAPS, GAPS Intro, AIP+

This soup flaunts fall flavors and ingredients. It's comfort food, and well-liked. Despite its general appeal, this soup is also classic healing food. It utilizes GAPS diet techniques that also happen to make the soup rich and delicious: Skin and fat get puréed with winter squash, optional sweet potato (great for AIP but omit for GAPS) and herbs to make a creamy broth base that exemplifies one of the secrets of our bone broth kitchen — that high-fat, nourishing bisque! The thickness of bisque bases can vary depending on the recipe and personal taste. This purée I left brothier, but that's flexible. Lastly, this soup starts with water instead of broth. Meat stock is created while the meat cooks.

Serves 6 to 8.

INGREDIENTS:

6 cups water

2 turkey thighs, whole, skin on, bone in (or use 6 to 8 chicken thighs and reduce meat's cooking time)

1 cooked butternut squash (see Recipe Notes). Set aside flesh from seed cavity and cube remaining squash from "neck" of squash or 1-1/2 pounds sweet potatoes, baked until fork tender and peeled. Cube half the sweet potatoes and reserve the other half to purée.

1 head cauliflower, chopped

1 onion, chopped

1 turnip, peeled and cubed (optional)

1/2 bunch of kale, chopped small

1/4 cup fat of choice (butter, coconut oil, bacon fat, lard or olive oil)

2 cloves garlic, minced or crushed

2 teaspoons dried sage

1 teaspoon dried thyme

1 teaspoon sea salt (and more, to taste)

1/4 teaspoon white pepper (omit for AIP)

INSTRUCTIONS:

1. Bring water to a simmer in a large stock pot. Place whole turkey thighs into water. Cover and simmer gently 20 minutes.

2. Add cauliflower, onion and turnip. Cover and simmer 15 minutes more.

3. Add kale. Simmer 5 minutes, uncovered.

4. Ladle out 3 cups broth to cool slightly.

5. Using tongs or slotted spoon, remove meat to a plate. Allow it to cool slightly. Reserve skin to one side and chop meat into bite-size pieces.

6. Add cooled broth to blender. Purée broth with the winter squash from around the seed cavity or half of the optional sweet potatoes, skin, fat, sage, thyme, sea salt and optional white pepper.

7. Return purée to pot. Add cubed winter squash or cubed sweet potatoes and garlic.

8. Stir, taste for sea salt, adding more as needed, and serve.

INSTANT POT INSTRUCTIONS:

1. Place 6 cups water and turkey thighs into Instant Pot. Seal lid, shut steam valve and press "Manual" button. Press "-" button until you reach 20 minutes.

2. When time has elapsed, press "Cancel" button. Allow pressure to release naturally for 1 hour. Carefully release any remaining steam. Remove lid.

3. Ladle out 3 cups broth to cool slightly.

4. Using tongs or slotted spoon, remove meat to a plate. Allow it to cool slightly. Reserve skin to one side and chop meat into bite-size pieces.

5. Press "Sauté" button on Instant Pot. To the broth in the Instant Pot, add cauliflower, onions and optional turnips. Cover with glass lid. Simmer without stirring 10 minutes.

6. Add kale. Cover again and allow to simmer 5 more minutes.

7. Press "Cancel" button twice, so "Keep Warm" setting turns on.

8. Add cooled broth to blender. Purée broth with the winter squash from around the seed cavity or half of the optional sweet potatoes, skin, fat, sage, thyme, sea salt and optional white pepper.

9. Return purée to pot. Add cubed winter squash or cubed sweet potatoes and garlic.

10. Stir, taste for sea salt, adding more as needed, and serve.

RECIPE NOTES:

See How to Bake Winter Squash on Page 149.

White Carrot Ginger Soup

Paleo, GAPS, GAPS Intro, AIP, VAD

This very simple soup combines savory and sweet. Savory stock combines with sweet carrots, earthy onions and spicy ginger. White carrots are often found in medley mixes of organic heritage carrots. Farmer's markets also sometimes offer them. For those on the VAD diet, they're a great crop to consider growing oneself. For those not on a VAD diet, orange or yellow carrots may also be used.

Serves 3 to 4 as a side dish, snack or light meal.

INGREDIENTS:

1-1/2 to 2-1/2 cups bone broth or meat stock (use more broth for a thinner soup and less for a thick bisque)
1 pound white carrots, roughly chopped
1 medium onion, roughly chopped
3- to 4-inch piece fresh ginger, cut into smaller pieces (use more for a spicier ginger flavor)
Garnishes: freshly grated ginger, crystallized ginger, diced sautéed onions, leftover chopped meat (optional)

INSTRUCTIONS:

1. Steam carrots and onions until very soft, about 25 minutes over simmering water.

2. While carrots steam, warm broth in large saucepan over medium heat. Do not allow it to simmer.

3. Place broth, carrots, onion and ginger in blender. (Use caution when blending hot liquids.) Purée on medium-high speed about 45 seconds until smooth.

4. Pour back into saucepan and heat until piping hot.

5. Pour into mugs or bowls. Drink and enjoy.

Beef Short Ribs
With White Peach and Apple Chutney

(an Instant Pot recipe)
Paleo, GAPS+, AIP, VAD

The gravy or sauce from which the short ribs emerge after cooking is one of my favorites. This stew can be made with or without the chutney. The chutney makes this meal super fresh and special. Without the fruit, this is just a great beef stew, good served with cauliflower rice or even by itself. Beef short ribs are the very best meat for a stew because they're incredibly moist, tender and flavorful. They cook in water, with other flavorful ingredients, and create a super rich meat stock. For the extra-gentle version of this recipe, don't broil the meat in the final step; otherwise, do.

Serves 4.

INGREDIENTS:

For Short Ribs:

2-1/2 to 3 pounds beef short ribs (4 ribs total)

2 onions, diced

2 cups water + 1/4 cup, divided use

2 tablespoons tapioca flour (not GAPS)

2 tablespoons garlic powder

1 tablespoon sea salt

1 tablespoon maple syrup (use honey for GAPS)

2 teaspoons dried ginger powder

4 cups cauliflower rice, cooked

For Chutney:

2 to 3 white peaches or nectarines, peeled and cut into 1/2-inch cubes

2 to 3 white-fleshed apples, peeled and cut into 3/4-inch cubes

1/4 cup water

juice of half a lime

1- to 2-inch piece fresh ginger, peeled and grated or minced, about 2 teaspoons

2 teaspoons maple syrup (use honey for GAPS)

1/4 teaspoon Ceylon cinnamon

INSTRUCTIONS:

For Short Ribs:

1. Combine in Instant Pot: beef, onions, 2 cups water, garlic powder, sea salt, maple syrup and ginger powder. Close lid and seal steam valve. Press "Stew" button and "+" button. Increase time to 60 minutes.

2. While short ribs are cooking, make the chutney (see below).

3. When timer goes off, press "Cancel" button. Do a quick release using a dish towel or hot pad for safety, or allow pressure to release naturally. Remove lid.

4. If you plan to broil the beef (optional — see step below), use a slotted spoon to transfer ribs to a cookie sheet or a broil-proof pan. Some of the bones may fall out, which is fine.

5. If you'd rather not broil, simply transfer ribs to another bowl or plate until the sauce has been thickened (see next step).

6. In a small bowl, stir together remaining water and tapioca flour until well mixed.

7. Press "Sauté" button on Instant Pot. When stock begins to simmer, add freshly stirred tapioca water and stir. Stock will thicken slightly within 1 to 2 minutes. Press "Cancel" button.

8. Serve when beef is broiled (see next step). If you chose not to broil, place beef short ribs back into sauce base briefly so they're warmed through.

9. Turn oven to Broil. Place short ribs on cookie sheet or in broil-proof pan. Place beef beneath burner for about 5 minutes. When fat is shiny and slightly caramelized, remove pan from oven.

For Chutney:

1. Place apples and water in small saucepan. Over medium heat, simmer 10 to 15 minutes, stirring occasionally, until apples are softened but still hold their shape.

2. While apples are simmering, combine remaining chutney ingredients in medium-size bowl: peaches, lime juice, ginger, maple syrup and cinnamon.

3. When apples are tender, add them to chutney bowl and fold the ingredients together well.

To serve:

1. Portion cauliflower rice into each dish (or use organic white Basmati rice for VAD).

2. Top with meat stock sauce and one short rib per dish.

3. Spoon chutney over the beef or to one side of the dish. Or serve chutney in a separate condiments dish with a spoon, and pass it at the table.

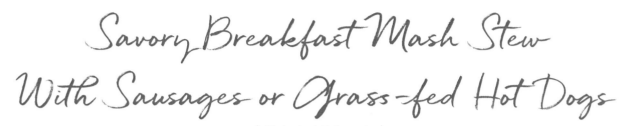

Savory Breakfast Mash Stew
With Sausages or Grass-fed Hot Dogs

(with Instant Pot version)
Paleo, GAPS, AIP, Keto, VAD

Years ago, when our family started the GAPS diet, our favorite breakfast was a big wedge of kabocha squash topped with butter and honey, (with a side of broth and protein). This recipe takes that idea and most people's love of mashed potatoes or sweet potatoes and creates a nourishing meal. A savory breakfast mash stew with a bone-broth-and-fat base is topped with fried sausages. A great way to start the day, and also delicious for a cozy dinner. The recipe's main vegetable ingredient varies depending on your diet. Those on a Paleo diet may use any of the vegetable options below. Otherwise, use the following guide:

GAPS diet: Choose winter squash.

AIP: Choose sweet potato, winter squash or cauliflower.

Keto: Choose cauliflower.

VAD: Choose mashed potato.

Serves 4.

INGREDIENTS:

3 pounds vegetable of choice: winter squash (peeled and seeds removed), russet potato (peeled), cauliflower (cored) or sweet potato (peeled) — all raw and roughly chopped

4 to 8 sausages (or high-quality grass-fed hot dogs, such as Applegate Farms), depending on how much meat your eaters eat, sliced or left whole according to preference

1-1/2 to 2 cups bone broth or meat stock

1/3 cup fat of choice: butter, ghee, coconut oil or schmalz (rendered chicken fat) + 2 teaspoons, divided use

3/4 teaspoon sea salt, or more, to taste

INSTRUCTIONS:

1. Place 1-1/2 cups broth and roughly chopped vegetables into large saucepan with fitted lid. Add 3/4 teaspoon sea salt, sprinkled over the vegetables. (Use only 1/2 teaspoon sea salt for sweet potatoes.) Cover pot. Simmer vegetables over medium heat until fork-tender, about 25 minutes.

2. While vegetables cook, fry up sausages: Heat a large cast-iron skillet over medium-high heat. Add 2 teaspoons fat to pan. Fry sausages whole or in slices. Rotate meat until browned evenly. Keep pan warm while you finish preparing the mash.

3. Turn off heat under saucepan.

4. Add 1/3 cup fat of choice to saucepan. Use a handheld mixer on the lowest speed to quickly create mash. Taste for salt. Russet potatoes might need more; sweet potatoes won't need any or very little. (Optionally, add more broth for a less thick mash and more bone broth benefits.)

5. Serve mash into each dish. Top with more fat if desired. Top with meat. Provide a side of fresh fruit if desired.

6. If not serving mash right away, keep sausages warm and saucepan over warm heat until ready to serve.

INSTANT POT INSTRUCTIONS:

1. Place 1-1/2 cups broth and roughly chopped vegetables into Instant Pot. Add 3/4 teaspoon sea salt, sprinkled over the vegetables. (Use only 1/2 teaspoon sea salt for sweet potatoes.) Seal lid and close steam valve. Press "Manual" button and "-" button. Decrease time to 10 minutes.

2. While vegetables cook, fry up sausages: Heat a large cast-iron skillet over medium-high heat. Add 2 teaspoons fat to pan. Fry sausages whole or in slices. Rotate meat until browned evenly. Keep pan warm while you finish preparing the mash.

3. When timer goes off, do a quick release. (Use a hot pad or dish towel to open the steam valve safely.)

4. Add 1/3 cup fat of choice to Instant Pot. Use a handheld mixer on the lowest speed to quickly create mash. Taste for salt. Russet potatoes might need more; sweet potatoes won't need any or very little. (Optionally, add more broth for a less thick mash and more bone broth benefits.)

5. Serve mash into each dish. Top with more fat if desired. Top with meat. Provide a side of fresh fruit if desired.

6. If not serving mash right away, keep sausages in Instant Pot on "Keep Warm" setting until ready to serve.

Apple Soup

GAPS, Paleo, VAD+

This cup is wonderful, healing, sweet, protein-rich goodness for an invalid. It's great for sore throats, for sick kids who don't want to eat much, for anyone who needs a cozy bowl but still wants a bit of protein and something that digests gently.

Serves 1.

INGREDIENTS:

1-1/2 cups water or mild-flavored broth or meat stock

1 large or 2 small apples, peeled and chopped (white-fleshed for VAD)

1 to 2 tablespoons slippery elm, (use 1 tablespoon for a thick apple cider texture; use 2 tablespoons for a thicker, more viscous, porridge-like texture)

1 to 2 tablespoons Paleo protein powder (see Recipe Notes) (optional for GAPS)

2 tablespoons collagen

1 teaspoon grated fresh ginger, or 1/8 teaspoon dried

1/8 teaspoon cinnamon (Ceylon cinnamon for VAD)

pinch of sea salt

INSTRUCTIONS:

1. Place apples and 1 cup water in small saucepan. Bring to a boil. Lower heat, and simmer gently for 15 minutes.

2. While apples simmer, whisk together dry ingredients in large bowl or mug: slippery elm, protein powder, collagen, cinnamon and sea salt.

3. Add only a small amount of the remaining 1/2 cup water to the dry ingredients, and whisk the powder into a paste. Add a bit more water, as needed, to wet all the ingredients. Add fresh ginger and any remaining water, stirring to mix.

4. When cooking time has elapsed and apples are tender, carefully pour them into the bowl or mug with spices, stirring as you pour until ingredients are well-mixed. Serve.

RECIPE NOTES:

See Resource Guide for links to the two Paleo protein powders I use, Page 162. One is beef-based, and one is egg-white-based.

dairy-free soups
and stews
[without nightshades, seeds or nuts]

CHAPTER TWO

Dairy-Free Soups and Stews

[Without Nightshades, Seeds or Nuts]

The recipes within this chapter fall mostly
under the following diets: Paleo, GAPS and AIP.
But you'll also find a couple of GAPS Intro, Keto and VAD recipes here.

Beef Tenderloin Skewers With Pineapple Stew

Paleo, GAPS+, AIP+, VAD

This soup makes a small portion. Double the recipe for a larger crowd. Pineapple Stew provides nice variety from veggie stews. It is like warm tropical salsa. This stew may also be served chilled or room temperature for hot-weather days, with a side of sizzling beef skewers.

Serves 3.

INGREDIENTS:

1 pound shaved beef steak or beef sirloin thinly sliced

1 pound fresh pineapple, diced or chopped small

1 large cucumber, peeled, de-seeded and diced or chopped small

1 cup sweet onion, diced

1 cup bone broth

1/4 cup grated fresh ginger

juice of 1 lime

2 cloves garlic, divided use

1 tablespoon + 2 teaspoons sesame oil, divided use (use avocado oil for AIP)

2 teaspoons coconut sugar (use honey for GAPS)

2 teaspoon maple syrup (not GAPS)

1-1/2 teaspoons sea salt, divided use

1/4 teaspoon cinnamon

Garnish: fresh probiotic cabbage sauerkraut

INSTRUCTIONS:

1. Soak 9 wooden skewers (8 to 10 inches long) in warm water for 15 to 20 minutes.

2. Grease a large cookie sheet with butter or avocado oil.

3. Marinate meat: In large bowl, stir together 1 tablespoon sesame oil, maple syrup, 1 clove garlic and 1/2 teaspoon sea salt. Add beef. Stir together well. Set aside.

4. Heat a large saucepan over medium heat. Add 2 teaspoons sesame oil, diced onions, 1 clove garlic and 1/2 teaspoon sea salt. Sauté until onions are softened and browned, about 10 minutes.

5. Turn heat to medium-low. Add broth, pineapple, cucumber, ginger, lime juice, remaining 1 clove garlic, coconut sugar (or honey), remaining 1/2 teaspoon sea salt and cinnamon. Stir together as the stew heats gently. Do not simmer.

6. When stew is very warm or just hot, reduce heat to lowest setting to keep warm while the meat cooks.

7. Set oven to broil and move an oven rack to the highest level.

8. Place beef on prepared skewers, leaving about 1-1/2 inches on each end. Line up skewers on greased cookie sheet.

9. Broil beef until cooked through (just beginning to char on the edges), about 10 minutes. Watch closely, checking on it occasionally.

10. Serve stew: Place skewers over the top edges to one side of each bowl. Garnish with optional fresh cabbage sauerkraut.

Thai Salmon Soup (Tom Kha Gai)

Paleo, GAPS, AIP, Keto, nightshade-free

Most people love Tom Kha Gai and are delighted to find it can be a simple-to-cook staple on many wellness diets. Feel free to omit or substitute an ingredient you may not be able to have to make this soup perfect for you and your family. Some examples include: I have omitted red bell peppers and chili pepper paste from this soup so it is nightshade-free and AIP. I love this soup with fresh salmon, whereas the soup can be (and usually is) made with chicken. The sweetener may be omitted. And for those who can't tolerate fruit or coconut, the coconut milk may be replaced with raw heavy cream if dairy is tolerated. (For those who want a more authentic spicy flavor and can tolerate nightshades, see Variation.)

Serves 4.

INGREDIENTS:

1 pound fresh salmon, skinned and boned, and cut into 8 equal portions (or you may use 2 cups shredded cooked chicken if you prefer)

3 cups bone broth, fish stock, shrimp stock or meat stock

14 ounces full fat coconut milk, or 1-3/4 cups

1 cup mushrooms, sliced

1 cup green onions, sliced diagonally

1 stalk lemongrass, halved lengthwise, or 1 drop lemongrass essential oil (see Recipe Notes)

2 tablespoons preferred fat (coconut oil, ghee, etc.)

2 tablespoons fresh ginger, grated

1 tablespoon + 1 teaspoon fish sauce

1 tablespoon coconut sugar (omit for Keto or add 5 drops liquid stevia or monk fruit to taste, for Keto)

4 cloves garlic, crushed or minced

1/2 teaspoon sea salt

Garnishes: 1/4 cup fresh cilantro, chopped, 1 lime, cut into wedges (or 2 tablespoons fresh lime juice)

INSTRUCTIONS:

1. Heat pan over medium heat. Add fat, mushrooms, whites of green onions and sea salt. Cook 3 minutes, stirring occasionally.

2. Add lemongrass, ginger and garlic, and stir again. Add broth or stock, coconut milk and sugar. Bring to a simmer. Reduce heat to medium-low. Simmer 10 minutes.

3. Add salmon and fish sauce. Cook over low heat about 5 minutes, until salmon is mostly cooked through.

4. Serve: Top with greens or green onions, fresh cilantro and lime wedges.

VARIATION:

For a non-AIP: Slice 1 red bell pepper thinly and add it with the salmon. Also add 1 to 2 teaspoons red Thai curry paste with the broth.

RECIPE NOTES:

See How to Use Fresh Lemongrass on Page 156.

See Resource Guide for a link to lemongrass essential oil, Page 162.

French Cabbage Soup With Bacon and Sausage

Paleo, GAPS, AIP+, Keto, VAD+

This soup was a customer favorite at our Paleo soup café. One of the ingredients that makes the soup's flavors come together so beautifully is the white pepper. If you're not on the AIP diet, I recommend using this ingredient; it's unique, special and distinctly different than black pepper. (I also give a good AIP alternative below.) French Cabbage Soup with Sausage and Bacon was inspired by a French savory pie I grew up eating at a special French restaurant. The soup has all the special comforting qualities of the pie with less work and, of course, no gluten. The VAD version omits both bacon and pork sausage (unless you've reintroduced pork) and uses ground turkey thigh instead.

Serves 6 to 8.

INGREDIENTS:

8 cups bone broth

2 pounds bulk pork (use ground turkey thigh for VAD)

6 ounces bulk bacon, already cooked, broken into 1-inch pieces (not VAD)

1 big head cabbage (about 3 pounds), cut and sliced finely into short strips

2 yellow onions, diced (use only 1 onion for Keto)

3-1/2 teaspoons sea salt, or less if your bone broth is salty, divided use

1/2 teaspoon white pepper or freshly ground black pepper (omit for AIP or replace white pepper with dried ginger)

INSTRUCTIONS:

1. Cook pork (or turkey for VAD) and 2 teaspoons sea salt over medium-high heat in a broad, deep pot, breaking up meat with a wooden or metal spatula. For ground turkey, add 2 tablespoons fat of choice to the pan before cooking. Cook until most of the pink is gone, about 10 minutes.

2. Using a slotted spoon, strain and set aside meat into a bowl, reserving fat in pan.

3. Place onions and 1 teaspoon sea salt in reserved fat over medium heat. Sauté 8 to 10 minutes, until translucent and softened. Add cabbage, white pepper and remaining sea salt.

4. Cover pan with lid to allow initial steam to wilt the cabbage. Reduce heat to medium-low. Cook 20 minutes, stirring occasionally.

5. Add bone broth and simmer 10 minutes. Add pork and bacon (or turkey for VAD) and cook an additional 10 minutes over low heat.

6. Serve with optional fresh chives or fresh parsley (not VAD).

Find recipes and insights at my blog,
EAT BEAUTIFUL
(www.eatbeautiful.net),
and Pinterest account
(https://www.
pinterest.com/
eatbeautifulnet/).

Roasted Carrot, Garlic and Thyme Bisque

Paleo, GAPS, AIP

Serves 4.

INGREDIENTS:

4 pounds carrots, whole and unpeeled

3 cups meat stock or bone broth, warm

1 large onion, sliced or chopped roughly

5 tablespoons bacon fat, melted, divided use (or use a combination of olive oil and coconut oil; if dairy isn't an issue, butter can be used)

2 bulbs garlic, separated into cloves

2 tablespoons fresh thyme leaves, or 1 teaspoon dried

1 teaspoon sea salt

INSTRUCTIONS:

1. Preheat oven to 350 degrees Fahrenheit.

2. Place carrots and chopped onions in two large casserole dishes, each dish with one tablespoon fat of choice, one bulb of garlic (separated into cloves) and 1/2 teaspoon sea salt. Using two spoons, toss to coat the carrots and onions in fat and sea salt.

3. Bake 1 hour. Allow to cool slightly.

4. While carrots and onions cool, peel (or squeeze out) the garlic cloves.

5. Place roasted vegetables in high speed blender. Add broth, 3 tablespoons remaining butter (or other fat), most of the garlic (reserve some for garnish) and thyme. Blend on medium-high speed 45 to 50 seconds, until completely smooth.

6. Pour into large saucepan. Heat over medium-high heat until very hot, without simmering.

7. Serve, topped with roasted garlic cloves and fresh thyme as optional garnishes.

VARIATION:

Serve topped with meatballs, for added protein and nutrition.

Beef Stew
With White Sweet Potatoes and Carrots

(an Instant Pot recipe) Paleo, GAPS+, AIP, VAD+

For the GAPS variation, simply omit the tapioca flour, and sub winter squash for the sweet potatoes and parsnips. For the VAD variation, use white potatoes and white carrots (if you can find them) and omit the parsley.

Serves 6 to 8.

INGREDIENTS:

2 pounds beef stew meat

1 pound parsnips, cut into 1/2- to 1-inch cubes (use winter squash for GAPS)

2 pounds carrots, sliced (use white carrots for VAD)

2 pounds white sweet potatoes, peeled and cut into cubes (use winter squash for GAPS; use white potatoes for VAD)

1 large onion, diced

4 cups broth + 1 cup additional broth (cold)

2 tablespoons tapioca starch (not GAPS)

2 teaspoons sea salt

2 teaspoons onion powder

2 teaspoons dried parsley (not VAD)

1-1/2 teaspoons garlic powder

1-1/2 teaspoons dried sage

Garnishes: fried garlic or freshly minced parsley (not VAD)

INSTRUCTIONS:

1. Layer ingredients in Instant Pot in the following order: broth, meat, sea salt, parsley, sage, parsnips, carrots, sweet potatoes, onion, onion powder, garlic powder. Press down slightly on all ingredients. (They should come to the maximum fill line in the 6-quart machine.)

2. Seal lid and close steam vent. Press "Stew" button and "+" button until 60 minutes is reached.

3. When timer goes off, allow pressure to release naturally for 1 hour.

4. Press "Keep Warm/Cancel" button twice. Cover steam vent with dish towel or hot pad, and open carefully.

5. Place remaining 1 cup cold broth in small saucepan. Thoroughly whisk in tapioca. Using a ladle, add about 3 cups hot broth to saucepan, continuing to stir.

6. Heat broth with tapioca on stovetop over medium heat, stirring the whole time, until sauce thickens.

7. Use a spatula to pour thickened broth into stew. Stir well until the stew base is evenly thick.

8. Taste for sea salt. Serve topped with optional fried garlic or freshly minced parsley (omit parsley for VAD).

Savoy Cabbage and Lemongrass Soup With Chicken, Mushrooms and Garlic

Paleo, GAPS+, GAPS Intro, AIP+, Keto

Fresh lemongrass is very easy to work with, but most of us aren't familiar with its preparation, so it seems intimidating. Or, we might not know where to buy it. I buy ours at a local Asian market. To prepare, you simply peel off the outer two to three layers, then chop off the bottom 12 inches or so. The inner heart or core of the stalk is what gets boiled, to add flavor to broths, soups and sauces. Alternatively, I often opt for lemongrass essential oil, which is incredibly convenient, because the flavor is so delicious and pungent, and I find that broth blended with lemongrass essential oil is very gentle and calming. Choose whichever option you prefer for this recipe. One other note about this recipe: It's a one-pot meal. This soup doesn't have a sauté stage, so there is one less step, one less pan to wash; it's easy and fast. Everything cooks in a large saucepan. We do use the blender. Note: This soup is both creamy and brothy. The photo doesn't show the broth.

Serves 6.

INGREDIENTS:

6 cups bone broth or meat stock

1-1/2 to 2 pounds boneless, skinless chicken thighs (about 6)

3 cups frozen and thawed or cooked cauliflower rice (about 12 ounces), or steamed cauliflower will work

2 onions, diced

1 cup coconut cream (or heavy, raw cream if dairy is tolerated)

5 ounces cremini mushrooms, diced

1/2 savoy cabbage, sliced thinly (about 3 to 4 cups)

2 stalks lemongrass, peeled, or 2 drops lemongrass essential oil (see Resource Guide)

1 large clove garlic

1 teaspoon sea salt

freshly ground black pepper, to taste, about 10 grinds (omit for AIP)

Garnishes: sautéed mushrooms, fried garlic slices and/or fresh chives (optional)

INSTRUCTIONS:

1. Place cauliflower, 2 cups broth and cream into blender. Set aside.

2. Prepare lemongrass for cooking (see Recipe Notes).

3. Place 4 cups broth in large saucepan. Add chicken thighs, onion, lemongrass (if using fresh) and black pepper. Bring to a boil, then reduce heat so broth gently simmers. Simmer uncovered 10 minutes.

4. Add mushrooms and 1 teaspoon sea salt, stirring to mix. Add cabbage on top; it doesn't need to be stirred in. Cover and simmer slowly for 20 minutes, reducing heat to medium-low as needed. (Take off the lid and stir once, after 10 minutes.)

5. After 20 minutes, reduce heat to lowest warm setting. Remove the lid.

6. Remove chicken to a large dish with tongs or slotted spoon. Add garlic to pot and stir.

7. Cut chicken into thin, small slices.

8. If using lemongrass essential oil, add it to the blender. Purée cauliflower 30 seconds, until smooth.

9. Pour purée into saucepan. Add chicken. Reheat, stirring, over medium heat until very hot throughout. Do not simmer.

10. Serve, optionally garnished with sautéed mushrooms, fried garlic and fresh chives.

Pho With Vegetable Noodles and Beef Short Ribs

(an Instant Pot recipe) Paleo, AIP+, GAPS+, GAPS Intro+, Keto, VAD+ {A "Dump and Cook" Recipe}

This soup is great for all the wellness diets in this book. Beef short ribs make the best pho base, rich in flavor and high in fat. We spice this broth with traditional star anise — or, for AIP and VAD, we use cloves, which is just as lovely and authentic for the well-loved Vietnamese traditional flavors of this soup. P.S. — Pho is pronounced "fuh" (rhymes with duh). :)

Serves 5.

INGREDIENTS:

6 cups + 1/4 cup water, divided use

2 to 2-1/2 pounds beef short ribs, 4 or 5 ribs

1 to 2 pounds zucchini or daikon radish, peeled and spiralized (see Resource Guide, Page 161, for recommended spiralizer)

1 pound baby bok choy, each "cabbage" cut in half or quarters lengthwise, depending on their size (or full-size bok choy, sliced thinly)

2 cups cremini mushrooms, sliced

12 ounces organic bean sprouts (optional, not GAPS Intro and AIP)

5-inch piece ginger root, grated or minced

6 cloves garlic, minced or crushed

1 handful of fresh spearmint leaves

2 tablespoons fish sauce (not VAD)

2 tablespoons tapioca flour (not GAPS)

1 tablespoon + 1/2 teaspoon sea salt, plus more if needed, to taste

1 tablespoon honey (or coconut sugar for non-GAPS)

3 whole star anise, or for AIP and VAD, use 1 teaspoon cloves (not GAPS Intro)

1 cinnamon stick about 3 to 4 inches long, or 1/2 teaspoon Ceylon cinnamon

INSTRUCTIONS:

1. Place water, beef and sea salt into Instant Pot. Add ginger, garlic, honey or coconut sugar, star anise or cloves and cinnamon. Seal lid and close steam valve. Press "Stew" button and use the "+" button to increase time to 60 minutes.

2. When timer goes off, do a quick pressure release or allow pressure to release naturally for 1 hour, according to preference. Carefully open steam valve and lid.

3. Use a slotted spoon to remove short ribs and any bones that have fallen out. Place ribs on large plate to cool slightly.

4. Press "Sauté" button. When broth begins to simmer, add bok choy and mushrooms. Simmer 3 minutes, stirring as needed so vegetables cook evenly.

5. Optional: While bok choy cooks, pull bones out of the short ribs, and remove any significant layers of fat or connective tissue. Cut or break meat into smaller pieces.

6. In a small bowl, stir together tapioca flour and water. Add freshly stirred tapioca water to simmering broth.

7. Add vegetable noodles to pot, and stir again. Cook 2 to 3 minutes, until broth is thickened and noodles are just-cooked, being careful not to overcook. (Daikon noodles are more forgiving and can cook longer than zoodles.)

8. Press "Cancel" button and use hot pads to remove insert from Instant Pot. Return meat to the pot. Stir in optional fish sauce. Taste for salt.

9. Serve, garnished with fresh mint and optional bean sprouts.

Hearty Nomato Beef Minestrone

Paleo, GAPS, AIP

I can't personally eat tomatoes, so I love, love, love this soup. It's everything hearty and delicious, packed with two kinds of meat, five herbs and so many veggies. Regarding the fresh rosemary, I love it; it tastes a bit like a pine forest, but more gourmet and fitting. Add less if you want just a hint of this herb, or add the greater quantity designated below if you want it to stand out a bit. If you have the Nomato Sauce ready ahead of time, this soup comes together quickly and easily. I like to make a big batch and keep it on hand.

Serves 4.

INGREDIENTS:

1 pound ground beef or lamb

12 ounces sausages (I use the lemongrass sausages from Niman Ranch. Also look at brands like Mulay's and Applegate Farms which make good, clean bratwurst and Italian Sausages.) For AIP, use 12 ounces bulk pork cooked up to avoid the pepper spices often found in ready-made sausages.

1 batch Nomato Sauce (about 5 cups): double the stovetop version or use the Instant Pot version (see Recipe Notes)

2 cups bone broth or meat stock

1 large onion, diced

1 cup celery, chopped

1 large fennel bulb, diced

2 carrots, sliced

16 ounces pearl onions, frozen and partially defrosted, each one cut in half (or 2 onions, diced)

2 to 4 tablespoons fresh rosemary, according to taste, chopped

2 tablespoons fat of choice

2 teaspoons sea salt

INSTRUCTIONS:

1. Heat large stockpot over medium-high heat. Add fat, diced onions, celery, fennel, carrots and 1 teaspoon sea salt. Sauté 10 minutes.

2. Add ground meat and remaining sea salt. Break meat up in pan as it cooks. Add Nomato Sauce and continue breaking up meat until it's in small pieces.

3. Stir in pearl onions. Reduce heat to medium, cover pan, and simmer 15 minutes, stirring occasionally.

4. Add broth and sausages. Simmer 5 additional minutes.

5. Stir in fresh rosemary, and serve.

RECIPE NOTES:

For Nomato Sauce: Double the stovetop version or use the Instant Pot version. See recipes on Page 159.

Vietnamese Shrimp Soup

(with Instant Pot version) Paleo, GAPS, AIP {A "Dump and Cook" Recipe}

Hot and renewing, this soup both comforts and nourishes. The stock is spicy from the ginger, invigorating from the lemongrass and good for weary souls. The soup cooks simply and quickly in a pot on the stove, or in an Instant Pot — no sautéing needed. If you'd like to forage more often, this soup has lovely greens in it and is a great place to begin or continue to use dandelion greens from your yard.

Serves 4 to 5.

INGREDIENTS:

6 cups warm meat stock (high fat)

1 pound raw large shrimp (prawns), frozen or defrosted (both OK); cut into 3 pieces each

1 to 2 drops lemongrass essential oil, or 2 tablespoons fresh lime juice

8 ounces shiitake mushrooms, caps removed, thinly sliced

4 cups winter squash, cubed (OK to use frozen), or white sweet potato (not GAPS)

1 cup frozen chopped spinach (or 3 cups fresh), partially defrosted to measure, or lots of freshly foraged dandelion greens, chopped

1/2 cup fresh cilantro or mint, chopped small

1/4 cup ginger, freshly grated or minced

3 tablespoons fish sauce

4 to 8 cloves garlic, crushed or minced

1/2 teaspoon sea salt, plus more to taste

INSTRUCTIONS:

1. Place 2 cups slightly cooled (warm) stock into blender. Add 1 to 2 drops essential oil. Put on lid and blend on lowest speed to start; then increase speed to medium for 10 seconds. (Use caution when blending hot liquids.) Omit this step if using fresh lime juice.

2. Place the blended broth and remaining 4 cups broth into large pot. Bring to a simmer over medium heat.

3. Add mushrooms, winter squash, ginger and garlic. Simmer 10 minutes over low heat.

4. Add the shrimp, fish sauce, spinach or dandelion greens and sea salt. Simmer 5 minutes more.

5. Turn off heat. Stir in fresh lime juice, if using.

6. Serve, topped with fresh cilantro or fresh mint.

INSTANT POT INSTRUCTIONS:

1. Place 2 cups slightly cooled (warm) stock into blender. Add 1 to 2 drops essential oil. Put on lid and blend on lowest speed to start; then increase speed to medium for 10 seconds. (Use caution when blending hot liquids.) Omit this step if using fresh lime juice.

2. Place the blended broth and remaining 4 cups broth into Instant Pot. Press the "Sauté" button and bring to a simmer over medium heat.

3. Add mushrooms, winter squash, ginger and garlic. Simmer 10 minutes over low heat.

4. Add the shrimp, fish sauce, spinach or dandelion greens and sea salt. Simmer 5 minutes more.

5. Press "Keep Warm" button on Instant Pot.

6. Stir in fresh lime juice, if using. Serve, topped with fresh cilantro or fresh mint.

Clams and Garlic in Broth

Paleo, GAPS, AIP+, Keto

If you've never made clams in broth, this dish is easy and its own special kind of comfort food. Growing up, this dish was always a favorite of mine. The clams themselves are delicious, and the broth is otherworldly.

Serves 6.

INGREDIENTS:

6 pounds small clams, littlenecks or cockles, soaked in cold water for 20 minutes, then drained just before cooking
2 cups bone broth
1/2 cup fresh parsley, minced
1/4 cup extra-virgin olive oil
2 slices bacon, diced with a sharp knife (small square pieces)
2 shallots, diced
5 cloves garlic, minced
1 teaspoon sea salt
1 teaspoon dried thyme
1/4 teaspoon red pepper flakes, optional (not AIP)
freshly ground black pepper, to taste (not AIP)
Garnish: 1 lemon, cut into wedges (optional)

INSTRUCTIONS:

1. In a large, broad saucepan over medium heat, cook bacon pieces until browned and most of the fat is rendered, 8 to 10 minutes.

2. Add olive oil to pan. Add shallots, garlic, sea salt, thyme, optional black pepper and optional red pepper flakes. Sauté 2 to 3 minutes.

3. Add clams and broth. Stir.

4. Increase heat to high and cover, bringing broth to a boil. Stir occasionally until clams open, about 5 to 7 minutes. Discard clams that do not at least partially open after 8 minutes.

5. Remove pot from heat. Top with fresh parsley.

6. Serve with optional lemon wedges.

Eggroll in a Bowl Soup

Paleo, GAPS, AIP, Keto+

The concept of Egg Roll in a Bowl has become popular — with its grain-free Asian comfort food flavors and textures, but none of the more difficult rolling or frying the wrapper. This recipe takes that idea to the healing soups level, and the result is delicious — plus, fast and easy to make.

Serves 4.

INGREDIENTS:

3 cups meat stock or bone broth

1 pound ground pork

1 large green cabbage, sliced thinly

1 large onion, peeled, cut in half and sliced lengthwise (use one bunch green onions for Keto, chopped)

3 carrots, about 1 cup, julienned or cut into matchsticks (omit for Keto, or replace with daikon radish)

1/4 cup coconut amino acids (or use 2 tablespoons real fermented soy sauce for Keto)

2 tablespoons toasted sesame oil, or avocado oil for AIP

1-inch piece fresh ginger, minced or grated

4 cloves garlic, minced or crushed

1 teaspoon sea salt

INSTRUCTIONS:

1. Heat oil in a large skillet over medium-high heat. Add the cabbage and sea salt. Sauté until tender, about 15 minutes. Remove cabbage to a large plate, and set aside.

2. Add pork and onion, breaking up meat into small pieces. Sauté until outside of meat is no longer pink — 10 minutes.

3. While pork is cooking, place broth in large saucepan and heat to simmering. Reduce heat, and keep warm.

4. Add carrots, fresh garlic, ginger and sea salt to pork and onions. Sauté until pork is cooked about 5 minutes.

5. Add cooked cabbage and coconut amino acids.

6. Use tongs or large serving spoon to serve into bowls.

7. To serve, ladle equal amounts of broth into each dish.

Sweet Breakfast Mash Stew With Berries and Ginger

(with Instant Pot version) Paleo, GAPS+, AIP+

This stew can be eaten any time of day, but it's a nice change for breakfast when you still want stew nutrition but with a creative and slightly sweet twist. Full of protein, fiber and complex carbs, this bowl is naturally sweet, with no added sweetener.

Serves 1 to 2.

INGREDIENTS:

1 large or 2 small sweet potatoes (not GAPS), or 1-1/2 to 2 cups cooked winter squash, baked and very hot (see Recipe Notes)

2 eggs, whisked and preferably room temperature (omit and skip egg instruction for AIP)

1/2 cup bone broth

1/4 cup coconut butter

2 tablespoons collagen powder

1 tablespoon coconut oil (or use butter or ghee if dairy is tolerated)

1/4 teaspoon cinnamon

sea salt, to taste

Optional toppings: berries, raisins or dried currants, dried coconut, grated fresh ginger, more coconut butter, etc.

INSTRUCTIONS:

1. Sweet potato version: Wash sweet potato. If sweet potato is large, chop in half. Insert knife into center so potato can release steam during cooking. Steam or bake sweet potato until very tender in the center and piping hot. (I bake mine on a cookie sheet at 375 degrees Fahrenheit for 1 hour.)

2. Shortly before sweet potato is done cooking, heat bone broth to a slow simmer in small saucepan.

3. Remove sweet potato and quickly peel.

4. Sweet potato or winter squash: In a medium-size bowl (or blender or food processor), mash sweet potato or hot winter squash and egg together. The hot potato will cook the egg. Add broth and mix again until smooth and the egg loses its gloss, about 1 minute.

5. Add remaining ingredients and stir again: coconut butter, collagen, ghee, cinnamon and sea salt.

6. Serve in bowl, and garnish with optional toppings: berries, raisins or dried currants, dried coconut, grated fresh ginger, more coconut butter, etc.

INSTANT POT INSTRUCTIONS:

1. Sweet potato version: Wash sweet potato. If sweet potato is large, chop in half. Insert knife into center so potato can release steam during cooking. Place trivet in Instant Pot and add 1 cup water. Press "Manual" button and "-" button to 20 minutes.

2. When timer goes off, press "Cancel" button. Place dish towel or hot pad over steam vent, and do a quick release.

3. Heat bone broth to a slow simmer in a small saucepan.

4. Quickly peel sweet potato.

5. Sweet potato or winter squash: In a medium-size bowl (or blender or food processor), mash sweet potato or hot winter squash and egg together. The hot potato will cook the egg. Add broth and mix again until smooth and the egg loses its gloss, about 1 minute.

6. Add remaining ingredients and stir again: coconut butter, collagen, ghee, cinnamon and sea salt.

7. Serve in bowl, and garnish with optional toppings: berries, raisins or dried currants, dried coconut, grated fresh ginger, more coconut butter, etc.

RECIPE NOTES:

See How to Bake Winter Squash on Page 149.

Cream of Cauliflower and Parsnip Soup

(an Instant Pot recipe) Paleo, AIP, VAD+ {A "Dump and Cook" recipe}

This soup's creaminess exemplifies how creamy a non-dairy soup can be with the use of fat (instead of cream) and the utilization of Secret #2 in Soup-Making Secrets (Page 130). This soup is also a good option for those who don't digest chicken (or other meat) well. The stock, skin and cartilage provide nourishing protein building blocks and are easier to digest. I like this soup for a cold, rainy, winter's night. Add grilled or cubed leftover chicken for protein if desired.

Serves 4.

INGREDIENTS:

1 head cauliflower, roughly chopped (use 2 peeled white russet potatoes for VAD)

1 large parsnip or two small (about 2 pounds), peeled and roughly chopped

3 cups broth

2 tablespoons fresh thyme leaves (use fresh rosemary for VAD)

1/2 cup leftover chicken skin and soft cartilage or 1/4 cup fat (see Recipe Notes)

1 clove garlic, peeled and chopped roughly

1/2 teaspoon sea salt

INSTRUCTIONS:

1. Place broth, cauliflower and parsnips into Instant Pot. Seal lid and press "Soup" button. Use "-" button to reduce time to 10 minutes.

2. When timer sounds, press "Cancel" button. Allow pressure to release naturally about 1 hour. (Or carefully open steam valve to do a quick release.) Carefully open steam valve. Remove lid.

3. Use a slotted spoon to remove solids to a medium-size bowl. Allow to cool about 30 minutes.

4. Place in blender: broth, vegetable solids, chicken skin and soft cartilage or 1/4 cup fat, garlic, sea salt and fresh herb. Purée until smooth, about 45 seconds on medium to medium-high speed. Blend only 20 to 25 seconds for VAD if using potatoes.

5. Pour back into Instant Pot for a brief reheating. Press "Sauté" button, and stir until soup is back to temperature. Press "Cancel" button when soup is hot.

6. Serve with garnishes: cubed grilled or leftover chicken and fresh herb of choice (thyme or rosemary for VAD).

RECIPE NOTES:

See Secret #2 in Soup Making Secrets: How to Use Fats in Soup, Page 130.

Visit my blog, E A T B E A U T I F U L (www.eatbeautiful.net/secrets-free-videos) to access Video #1 and #2.

*See Bonus Video #1
to watch me share the
"How to Use Fats in Soup"
concept from
Soup Making Secrets.*

Trotters, Neck or Beef Tail Curry

(an Instant Pot recipe) Paleo, GAPS+, AIP+, Keto+, VAD {A "Dump and Cook" Recipe}, nightshade-free

Trotters are high-fat leg bones or hooves. They're delicious, rich with fat, gelatin and flavor — and wonderful for wellness diets. Beef tail and neck have similar qualities. I love nothing more than a high-fat, fall-apart meat stew curry, so this Trotter, Neck or Beef Tail Curry is my cup of tea. See what your butcher has: Look for lamb or goat trotters, but beef is good, too. A lot of curries contain nightshades, so I've made this one nightshade-free for those of us who love curry but can't have nightshades. One of the benefits of using the Instant Pot is we don't need to brown stew meat before a long cooking. The rich, deep flavor comes anyway. The high heat of the Instant Pot promotes caramelization and complex flavors (with less work). We also end up with tender, juicy meat.

Serves 4 to 5.

INGREDIENTS:

2 to 5 pounds trotters, neck bones with meat or beef tail

6 zucchini, peeled, de-seeded and chopped

3 cups cauliflower rice (sub minced or grated white potatoes or parsnips for VAD)

2 cups + 1/4 cup water, divided use

2 to 4 teaspoons sea salt (ratio: use 3/4 to 1 teaspoon sea salt for every pound of meaty bones you use; for 5 pounds of meat, use 4 teaspoons sea salt)

1/4 cup tapioca flour (not GAPS and Keto)

1 tablespoon dried ginger

2 teaspoons cumin (not AIP)

2 teaspoons onion powder

1-1/2 teaspoons garlic powder

1-1/2 teaspoons turmeric

1/2 teaspoon cinnamon

INSTRUCTIONS:

1. Place bones and 2 cups water into Instant Pot. Add sea salt, optional cumin, ginger, onion, garlic, turmeric and cinnamon. Lock lid and seal steam valve. Press "Stew" button and "+" button to 60 minutes.

2. When timer goes off, allow 1 hour for pressure to release naturally.

3. Press "Cancel" button. Carefully open steam valve. Remove lid.

4. Use slotted spoon to remove meat and bones to a large bowl or plate.

5. Press "Saute" button. When stock begins to simmer, add cauliflower rice and zucchini. Simmer 5 to 10 minutes.

6. Remove 3 cups fatty broth and vegetable solids. Allow to cool slightly.

7. Whisk together tapioca with remaining 1/4 cup water. Add freshly stirred tapioca water to simmering stew. Stir until stew base thickens slightly, about 1 minute.

8. Press "Cancel" button twice to set Instant Pot base to "Keep Warm" setting.

9. Remove bones from the meat you've set aside. Add meat back to stew base.

10. Add cooled stock and vegetables to blender. (You can also add any extra fat or connective tissue from the meat and bones, if desired.) Purée until smooth, about 15 seconds. Pour back into stew. Stir gently.

11. Serve stew with fried potatoes, steamed rice, smashed cauliflower, fried parsnips or other favorite side dish that fits your dietary guidelines.

Parsnip and Mushroom Soup With Pork and Bacon

Paleo, AIP+

This soup is rich and flavorful. If you don't love parsnips yet, I hope this soup will bring you around.

Serves 5.

INGREDIENTS:

3 cups meat stock or bone broth

1 pound bulk ground pork

3 large parsnips, peeled and chopped

3 large onions, peeled and roughly chopped

5 to 6 ounces shiitake mushrooms

1/2 pound bacon

1/4 cup bacon fat or rendered pork lard

3 tablespoons fresh thyme, plus more for garnish

2 tablespoons preferred traditional fat (ghee, butter, lard or bacon fat)

1 tablespoon dried parsley

2 teaspoons sea salt + 1/2 teaspoon

1/4 teaspoon white pepper (not AIP)

INSTRUCTIONS:

1. Preheat oven to 350 degrees Fahrenheit.

2. Place bacon fat, parsnips, onions and 2 teaspoons sea salt into two roasting pans, evenly divided use (2 tablespoons fat and 1 teaspoon sea salt per pan). Toss to coat. Bake parsnips and onions 45 minutes to 1 hour, until tender and toasty brown. When done, transfer half the parsnips to a plate. Place plate in warm oven. (Watch parsnips closely and remove from oven sooner as needed.)

3. While veggies roast, sauté mushrooms. Heat 2 tablespoons preferred fat in large skillet. When hot, add mushrooms. Sprinkle remaining 1/2 teaspoon sea salt evenly over mushrooms. Cook over high heat 3 to 5 minutes, stirring occasionally.

4. Reduce heat to medium and cook an additional 3 to 5 minutes, until mushrooms are wilted, toasty and fragrant.

5. Place the following in a high-powered blender: 3 cups broth, all the roasted onions, half the roasted parsnips (the ones remaining in the roasting pan), fresh thyme, dried parsley and white pepper. Use a spatula to scrape fat from roasting pans into blender.

6. Purée 30 seconds on medium speed, or until smooth. Pour purée into large saucepan. Heat over high heat until purée begins to simmer. Reduce heat to medium.

7. Add bulk pork, and immediately start breaking it up in the pot into small pieces. Cook about 8 minutes until all pork is in small and tiny pieces and is cooked through.

8. Taste soup for salt. Add up to 1 teaspoon if needed.

9. Serve soup, topping each bowl with sautéed mushrooms, bacon, reserved warm parsnips and generous amounts of fresh thyme.

VARIATION:

If seeds are tolerated (not AIP): This soup was originally made in our soup café with toasted sesame oil. The shiitake mushrooms and sesame oil made an Asian-themed soup that customers loved. If you can have seeds and you like the idea, sub toasted sesame oil for up to 1/4 cup of the fat used elsewhere in this recipe, and omit the thyme. Also add 1/4 cup tahini and 1 clove of garlic to the blender purée. Both versions are lovely; so make what sounds good.

Chicken Pot Pie Baked Stew

Paleo, AIP

This stew bakes in a casserole dish, topped with savory biscuits. The nutrient-dense gravy can be made ahead of time to make the assembly of the casserole faster and easier:

Step 1 — Make gravy. (Gravy may be made ahead by up to three days and kept in the fridge until you're ready to assemble the casserole.)

Step 2 — Assemble casserole.

Step 3 — While the casserole goes through an initial baking, make the biscuit dough.

Step 4 — Top casserole with biscuits and complete baking of stew.

Serves 8 to 10.

INGREDIENTS:

For Gravy:

3 large onions, diced

1 cup creamy coconut milk

1 cup bone broth or meat stock

3 tablespoons lard, bacon fat or avocado oil

3 slices bacon

1/2 ounce dried mushrooms (optional), soaked in hot water for 15 minutes

3 cloves garlic

3/4 teaspoon dried sage

3/4 teaspoon dried thyme

3/4 teaspoon sea salt

For Biscuits:

1-1/2 cups cassava flour (spoon flour into measuring cup, then slide extra off the top with the back of a knife)

1 cup water or coconut milk, cold

1/2 cup solid fat (cold or cold-room temperature): lard or palm shortening (not Spectrum brand; see Recipe Notes)

1/4 cup collagen

1 tablespoon apple cider vinegar or sauerkraut juice (if no-fruit diet)

1/2 teaspoon baking soda, sifted

1/4 teaspoon sea salt

For Casserole:

1 batch gravy

1 batch biscuits (recipe follows)

2 pounds skinless, boneless chicken thighs, chopped into 6 pieces each

2 large onions diced, or 1 bag frozen pearl onions

4 large carrots, cut diagonally

1 10-ounce bag frozen peas (optional for AIP)

2 tablespoons fat of choice: lard, bacon fat, coconut oil or avocado oil

2 teaspoons dried thyme

1 teaspoon sea salt

Garnish: fresh sage or thyme leaves

INSTRUCTIONS:

For Gravy:

1. Melt fat in a large skillet over medium-high heat. Add onions, bacon and sea salt, stirring occasionally until onions are just wilted and starting to brown, 5 to 8 minutes.

2. Reduce heat to low and cover, stirring every 5 to 10 minutes, for 20 minutes total.

3. Add the garlic and herbs. Sauté an additional 5 minutes, until fragrant.

4. Add coconut milk, bone broth and optional dried (soaked) mushrooms, de-glazing the pan as you stir.

5. Simmer, uncovered over medium-high heat, 5 minutes more, reducing down overall liquid.

6. Turn off heat. Allow to cool slightly.

7. Spoon 3/4 of the mixture into a blender, including both bacon pieces, and purée 15 to 20 seconds at medium-high speed.

8. Stir purée back into remaining gravy in pan. Heat gently, stirring.

9. Gravy is now ready for use in the stew, or refrigerate for up to three days before assembling.

For Biscuits:

1. Combine water and apple cider vinegar in small dish. Set aside.

2. In large bowl, whisk together dry ingredients: cassava flour, collagen, sea salt and baking soda. Set aside.

3. Cut fat into flour using a food processor, pastry blender or two knives. Pulse to combine until largest fat pieces are pea-size.

4. Pour water and apple cider vinegar into flour mixture, and stir to just combine. Do not over-mix. (I use no more than 15 strokes with my rubber spatula.)

5. If using cut biscuits, dump dough out onto parchment lined cookie sheet. Form into a 2-inch thick rough square. Do not pat it down. (Dumping out dough is optional; a cookie dough scoop can also be used.)

6. Using a sharp knife, cut straight down into dough. Dip knife in flour after each cut, until you have all biscuits cut. (Or, once again, use a large cookie scoop to portion dough.)

7. Spread separate biscuits evenly out over casserole surface. Follow baking instructions from casserole recipe (see next steps).

For Casserole:

1. Grease a large casserole dish, 9-inch-by-13-inch or larger. Add raw chicken thigh pieces, somewhat equally spaced apart. Set aside.

2. Preheat oven to 375 degrees Fahrenheit.

3. Heat large skillet over high heat until pan is hot. Add fat. Add onions and sea salt. Sauté 8 to 10 minutes.

4. Add carrots and dried thyme. Sauté an additional 5 minutes.

5. Ladle onions and carrots over raw chicken. Add frozen peas. Add gravy, pouring it evenly over ingredients.

6. Place casserole dish in preheated oven for 40 minutes, while you make the biscuit dough (see next steps).

7. When biscuit dough is complete, either use a large cookie scoop to forms mounds of dough or cut biscuits into squares. Do not over-mix; follow biscuit guidelines for scooping or cutting.

8. Remove hot casserole dish from oven. Increase oven temperature to 400 degrees.

9. Place portioned biscuit batter over the surface of casserole contents. There will be spaces between each biscuit.

10. Bake in 400 degree oven 25 to 30 (additional) minutes, until edges are bubbly, center is very hot and a bit bubbly, and biscuits are tinged with brown and golden.

11. Remove from heat, and garnish with fresh sage or fresh thyme. (Fresh sage begins to brown when heated, so garnish directly before serving.)

12. Serve.

RECIPE NOTES:

If you use palm shortening, look for solid palm shortening (one ingredient and sustainably sourced), such as Grain Brain Organic Palm Oil Shortening. See Resource Guide for a link, Page 162.

Visit my blog, E A T B E A U T I F U L (www.eatbeautiful.net/secrets-free-videos) to access Video #1 and #2.

See Bonus Video #2 to watch me share the "How to Use Herbs in Soup" concept from Soup Making Secrets.

Spiced Lamb Stew With Sweet Potatoes

(an Instant Pot recipe) Paleo, AIP+ {A "Dump and Cook" Recipe}

Slow-cooked lamb with spices like star anise, served on mashed sweet potatoes. See the AIP spice variations below.

Serves 4 to 6.

INGREDIENTS:

2 pounds lamb shoulder, cubed, or lamb stew meat (lamb shoulder is more tender and "special"; lamb stew meat is more affordable and works fine)

4 whole sweet potatoes, washed and unpeeled

2 large onions, peeled and chopped

2 cups water

2 tablespoons coconut oil

2-1/2 teaspoons sea salt

2 teaspoons cumin (for AIP, sub 2 teaspoons dried ginger)

1 teaspoon allspice (for AIP, sub 1/2 teaspoon cinnamon + 1/2 teaspoon mace + 1/8 teaspoon cloves)

4 whole star anise pieces (not AIP)

INSTRUCTIONS:

1. Place all ingredients (except 2 tablespoons coconut oil) into Instant Pot, reserving the sweet potatoes to place on the very top. Seal lid. Close steam valve. Press "Stew" button and "+" button to increase time to 60 minutes.

2. When time has elapsed, press "Keep Warm/Cancel" button. To do a quick release, cover steam valve with a dish towel or hot pad. Carefully open valve. Or do a slow-release, allowing 1 hour for pressure to release. Remove lid.

3. Use a slotted spoon or tongs to remove sweet potatoes to a plate to cool.

4. When cool enough to handle, peel potatoes and mash (use handheld mixer, mash by hand or place in food processor or blender with remaining 2 tablespoons coconut oil).

5. To serve, place equal amounts of sweet potato in each dish. Give lamb stew a stir. Spoon it over the sweet potatoes.

Healthy Chocolate Soup

Paleo, GAPS+, AIP+, Keto+, VAD+

Like a warm, nourishing smoothie in a bowl or mug. (You don't taste the broth or cauliflower. My family had no idea until I told them.)

Serves 3 to 4.

INGREDIENTS:

2 cups bone broth or meat stock

1 head of cauliflower, roughly chopped (use 2 pounds peeled parsnips for VAD)

5 tablespoons carob or fair trade cocoa powder (carob for AIP and initial detox stage of VAD, cocoa for GAPS)

5 tablespoons maple syrup (use honey for GAPS; use stevia or pure monk fruit to taste for Keto, or use a combination of stevia and Lakanto maple syrup for Keto; use part maple syrup + stevia to taste for VAD, if desired)

1/4 cup coconut oil (or butter, if dairy is tolerated)

2 tablespoons collagen (optional)

Garnishes: fresh or frozen berries, cocoa nibs (not AIP)

Optional add-ins: cordyceps mushroom powder (best if you're eating this soup in the morning or afternoon for a boost of energy)

INSTRUCTIONS:

1. Steam cauliflower until very soft, about 15 to 20 minutes over simmering water.

2. While cauliflower steams, warm broth in large saucepan. Do not allow to simmer or get too hot.

3. Place broth, cauliflower, carob or cocoa, maple syrup (other sweetener), coconut oil (or butter) and optional collagen into blender. (Use caution when blending hot liquids.) Purée on medium-high speed for about 45 seconds until smooth.

4. Pour back into saucepan and heat until piping hot.

5. Pour into mugs or bowls. Drink and enjoy.

dairy-free soups and stews
[with nightshades, seeds or legumes]

CHAPTER THREE

Dairy-Free Soups and Stews
[With Nightshades, Seeds or Legumes]

Most of the recipes in this chapter fall under these diets:

Paleo, GAPS and Keto. However, the first recipe in the chapter is AIP+.

Chicken and Apple Soup With Paprika, Sage and Chives

Paleo, GAPS, AIP+

This recipe makes a meat stock as the soup cooks, so you can start without any broth.

Serves 8 to 10.

INGREDIENTS:

8 cups filtered water

4 pounds chicken thighs, bone in, skin on

2 large onions, diced

2 leeks, greens included, cut in half lengthwise

3 large apples, peeled and cubed, preferably Granny Smith or other tart variety

5 teaspoons + 1-1/2 teaspoons sea salt, divided use

2 teaspoons paprika (not AIP)

2 teaspoons thyme

2 teaspoons dried sage

2 tablespoons olive oil, or preferred fat

Garnish: fresh herbs, such as parsley or chives (optional)

INSTRUCTIONS:

1. Place chicken in large pot with 8 cups water and 5 teaspoons sea salt. Bring to a boil, then reduce heat to a slow simmer. Cover and cook 30 minutes, until chicken is cooked through and a stock is made.

2. Use a slotted spoon to remove chicken to a plate to cool.

3. When chicken is cooled, remove skin and bones, reserving skin. Place skin in blender. Chop chicken into bite-size pieces. Set aside.

4. Bring broth back to a simmer. Add leeks. Cover and cook 8 minutes. Turn off heat. Allow to cool 1 hour.

5. Use slotted spoon to scoop up leeks and to place leeks in blender. Add about 3 cups broth, paprika, thyme and sage. Purée 30 seconds on medium speed, until purée is smooth.

6. To a large skillet, add fat of choice, diced onions, apples and 1-1/2 teaspoons sea salt. Cook 10 minutes over medium-high heat, until onions are softened and beginning to brown.

7. Add leek purée and remaining broth from pot. Bring to simmer and cook 20 minutes.

8. Add chicken, and turn off heat.

9. Serve, garnished with fresh minced parsley or chives.

Yellow Split Pea Soup

(with Instant Pot version) GAPS, VAD

This soup reminds me of my vegetarian days ... eating a lot of delicious curries. I've made the curry spices here nightshade-free. Pressure cooking helps to make yellow split peas more digestible. Bone broth adds protein and nutrition to this soup. Yellow Split Pea Soup is also delicious fortified with cooked ground beef and/or roasted cauliflower (Page 148). For those who can have fried potatoes or white rice (VAD), those are nice additions to serve to one side of the soup, which becomes quite stew-like as it cools. This soup is virtually A "Dump and Cook" Recipe, with just a bit of sautéing first — very easy to make, filling and satisfying to eat.

Serves 6.

INGREDIENTS:

6 cups bone broth

2 cups yellow split peas, rinsed and picked over

1 medium white onion, peeled and diced

1 bulb fennel, diced

4 stalks celery, diced

1/4 cup fresh ginger, minced

1 tablespoon fat of choice

5 cloves garlic, peeled and minced

1-1/2 teaspoons ground cumin

1-1/2 teaspoons ground ginger

1/2 teaspoon turmeric

1/4 teaspoon cinnamon

sea salt to taste (up to 1-1/2 teaspoons)

Garnishes: freshly ground black pepper, fried or roasted potatoes, freshly squeezed lemon juice (optional)

INSTRUCTIONS:

1. Heat fat in a large stockpot over medium-high heat. Add fat of choice, onion, fennel and celery. Sauté for 5 minutes, stirring occasionally, until the onions are softened and translucent.

2. Add ginger and garlic and sauté for 1 more minute, stirring occasionally, until fragrant.

3. Stir in bone broth, split peas and spices until combined. Continue cooking until the soup reaches a simmer. Cover and cook over lowered heat (maintain a slow simmer) for 40 minutes, stirring occasionally, until the split peas are completely tender.

4. Add sea salt, to taste and stir. Soup will thicken as it cools a bit.

5. Garnish and serve.

INSTANT POT INSTRUCTIONS:

1. Press "Sauté" button on Instant Pot. Add fat of choice, onion, fennel and celery. Sauté for 5 minutes, stirring occasionally, until onions are softened and translucent.

2. Add ginger and garlic and sauté for 1 more minute, stirring occasionally, until fragrant.

3. Stir in bone broth, split peas and spices until combined.

4. Seal lid and close steam valve. Press "Cancel" button, then press "Soup" button and "-" button to reach 18 minutes.

5. When timer goes off, allow pressure to release naturally for 15 minutes. Carefully open the steam release knob to quick release the remaining pressure.

6. Add sea salt, to taste and stir. Soup will thicken as it cools a bit.

7. Garnish and serve.

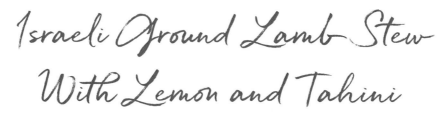

Israeli Ground Lamb Stew With Lemon and Tahini

Paleo, GAPS, Keto

With most stews, everyone gets served two ladlefuls, or more. This stew is rich and a lot like warm hummus (big heart eyes!). It serves four, with each person receiving one ladleful of stew to start. The stew is topped with spiced lamb and pairs well with any Middle Eastern toppings or sides you have: shredded lettuce, cucumbers, roasted peppers, olives, lemon wedges, grain-free flatbread, etc.

Serves 3 to 4.

INGREDIENTS:

3 cups (+ up to 1 cup more) broth or meat stock (see Recipe Notes)

1 pound ground lamb

2 medium-size onions, diced (use only 1 onion or sub fennel for Keto)

8 ounces pine nuts, raw and soaked 4 to 6 hours (see Recipe Notes)

6 tablespoons extra-virgin olive oil or butter, divided use

2 tablespoons fresh lemon juice or 2 drops lemongrass essential oil

1/4 cup hulled tahini

1/4 cup fresh parsley, minced

4 cloves garlic, crushed or minced, divided use

2 teaspoon dried oregano

3/4 teaspoon cumin, divided use

1/2 teaspoon onion powder

2 teaspoons sea salt + additional 1/2 teaspoon, to taste

Garnishes and sides: fresh parsley, shredded lettuce, cucumbers, roasted peppers, olives, lemon wedges, grain-free flatbread, additional pine nuts, green onions, turmeric, etc.

INSTRUCTIONS:

1. Heat large saucepan over medium-high heat. Add 2 tablespoons olive oil or butter, onions and 1 teaspoon sea salt. Sauté 5 minutes.

2. Meanwhile heat skillet over medium-high heat. Add lamb and remaining 1 teaspoon sea salt. Cook lamb, stirring and breaking up meat for about 3 minutes, until lamb begins to brown.

3. Add oregano, onion powder and 1/4 teaspoon cumin. Cook an additional 5 minutes, continuing to break meat up in pan. Remove from heat.

4. Stir in 1 clove of garlic. Keep warm in oven on lowest heat setting.

5. After 5 minutes of cooking onions in saucepan, add 3 cups broth. Simmer 10 minutes over medium heat.

6. Stir in remaining 3 cloves garlic. Set aside to cool slightly, about 10 minutes.

7. Place the following in blender: soaked pine nuts, broth and onion mixture, tahini, remaining olive oil or butter (4 tablespoons), lemon juice or lemongrass essential oil and remaining 1/2 teaspoon cumin. Blend on medium speed about 25 seconds.

8. Open the lid and check the thickness and taste. Add 1/2 teaspoon sea salt, as needed. Add more broth if you want the purée thinner. (I like mine thick, more like hummus.) Blend again briefly.

9. Pour purée back into saucepan. Reheat over medium heat, stirring, until steaming hot but not simmering.

10. To serve, ladle purée into shallow bowls. Scoop lamb on top or to the side.

11. Garnish with lemon wedges, freshly minced parsley and any other Middle Eastern items you enjoy and your diet allows, such as cucumbers, jicama slices (not GAPS), shredded romaine, olives, roasted red peppers, etc.

RECIPE NOTES:

See Meat Stock recipe on Page 136.
See How to Soak Seeds or Nuts on Page 155.

Japanese Udon Soup

Paleo, GAPS, AIP+, Keto

In my late 20s, I worked as a kitchen chef in a high-end Seattle sushi bar restaurant. I got the job so I could learn how to make authentic broths and Japanese mainstays. (I loved reading cookbooks to learn, but Japanese cooking felt elusive without learning foreign techniques and ingredients from a chef in person.) I have vivid memories from that year in a tiny kitchen with several unique Japanese men trying to figure out what to do with the first woman they had ever taught to cook sacred Japanese staples. Bonito is a staple stock used as a base in many Japanese dishes, and udon is a noodle dish eaten by natives. While Seattle natives ate plates of raw fish, our native Japanese customers almost always ordered udon soup. This recipe models the look and many of the ingredients of that authentic dish, but the ingredients are modified to be healthier and grain-free. Instead of feeling one's eyes glaze over (which mine used to do) after finishing a huge bowl of gluten-rich udon noodles, this bowl of daikon noodles with rich broth and greens should leave you feeling full and energized, also warmed through and comforted. (The miso is optional.)

Serves 4.

INGREDIENTS:

2 to 3 pounds daikon radish, peeled and spiralized (see Recipe Notes)

6 cups bonito stock), bone broth or meat stock (see Recipe Notes)

10 ounces fresh kale or spinach

4 eggs, poached or fried (see Recipe Notes)

1/2 cup water

4 ounces shiitake mushrooms, stems cut off and sliced

3 tablespoons white miso, optional (not AIP)

2 tablespoons coconut amino acids

1 tablespoon toasted sesame oil (not AIP) or avocado oil

1/4 teaspoon sea salt

Optional meat of choice: cooked shrimp, sautéed shaved beef or thinly sliced pork tenderloin

Optional garnishes: radishes cut out with tiny cookie cutters, microgreens, sesame seeds (not AIP)

INSTRUCTIONS:

1. Bring broth to a simmer in medium-large saucepan.

2. Place miso and coconut amino acids in 2-cup mixing bowl or measuring cup.

3. While broth heats, bring 1/2 cup water to a simmer in large frying pan. Add kale or spinach. Sauté over medium heat until greens are completely wilted. Cook longer for kale. Add more water if needed. When water has evaporated and greens are well-wilted, remove them to a dish to cool slightly.

4. Add 1 tablespoon sesame oil or avocado oil to pan. Add mushrooms and sea salt. Sauté 5 minutes over medium-high heat, until wilted and beginning to brown. Remove from heat.

5. When broth comes to a simmer, add daikon noodles. Simmer 4 minutes — no longer.

6. Ladle broth and use tongs to add noodles to each dish. Top with a poached egg.

7. Using your hands, gently squeeze out any water from the kale or spinach, and form 4 small tight handfuls of greens. Place one ball of greens in each dish.

8. Serve 1/4 of the mushrooms to one side of each dish. Add optional meat.

9. Garnish with optional toppings: radishes cut out with tiny cookie cutters, microgreens or sesame seeds (omit for AIP).

RECIPE NOTES:

See Meat Stock on Page 136.

See Bone Broth on Page 138.

See Bonito Stock on Page 141.

See How to Poach or Fry Eggs on Page 154.

See Resource Guide for a link to my favorite spiralizer, Page 161.

Indian Lamb Curry

(with Instant Pot version) Paleo, GAPS, Keto

I love a lot of stews and soups, but there aren't any that I love more than lamb curry. Lamb stew meat is the perfect choice on a tight budget. If you want to splurge, use lamb shoulder.

Serves 4 to 6.

INGREDIENTS:

2 pounds lamb stew meat, cubed

28 to 32 ounces canned tomatoes, diced

4 cups fresh spinach, chopped or 1 cup frozen spinach

2 cups bone broth or meat stock

2 large onions, diced (use only 1 onion for Keto version or sub fennel)

8 garlic cloves, minced or crushed

4 bay leaves

1/4 cup currants (optional)

2 tablespoons avocado oil or ghee

2-inch piece of ginger, minced or grated

1 tablespoon sea salt

1 tablespoon + teaspoon ground cumin

3 teaspoons ground coriander

1 teaspoon ground turmeric

1 teaspoon paprika

1 teaspoon chili powder

1 teaspoon garam masala

1/4 teaspoon cloves powder

1/4 teaspoon cardamom

1/4 teaspoon cinnamon

Additional accompaniments: fresh mint, cilantro and yogurt

INSTRUCTIONS:

1. Heat large Dutch oven or deep skillet with lid over high heat. Add fat, onions and 1 teaspoon sea salt. Reduce heat to medium high. Sauté 8 to 10 minutes, until softened and beginning to brown.

2. Add spices: cumin, coriander, turmeric, paprika, chili powder, garam masala, cloves, cardamom, cinnamon and bay leaves. Sauté 2 minutes more, until spices are fragrant.

3. Add lamb, broth, tomatoes, remaining 2 teaspoons sea salt, ginger and garlic. Stir. Cover and simmer over medium-low heat 1-1/2 to 2 hours, until meat is tender and falling apart.

4. Stir in spinach until it's wilted and hot.

5. Serve, garnished with optional currants (not Keto). May also be garnished with fresh mint, cilantro and yogurt (or cultured cream for Keto).

INSTANT POT INSTRUCTIONS:

1. Press "Sauté" button on Instant Pot. Add fat, onions and 1 teaspoon sea salt. Sauté about 8 minutes, until softened and beginning to brown.

2. Add spices: cumin, coriander, turmeric, paprika, chili powder, garam masala, cloves, cardamom, cinnamon and bay leaves. Sauté 2 minutes more, until spices are fragrant.

3. Add lamb, broth, tomatoes, remaining 2 teaspoons sea salt, ginger and garlic. Stir. Cover with lid and seal. Check that steam valve is shut. Select "Stew" button. Increase time using the "+" button until time reaches 60 minutes.

4. When timer sounds, allow pressure to release naturally for 30 minutes. Then press "Cancel" button.

5. Open steam valve carefully using a hot pad or dish towel. Open lid.

6. Stir in spinach until it's wilted and hot.

7. Serve, garnished with optional currants (omit for Keto). May also be garnished with fresh mint, cilantro and yogurt (or cultured cream for Keto).

Italian Stuffed Pepper Soup

(with Instant Pot version) Paleo, GAPS, Keto

This recipe makes a nice big batch. If you make it in the 6-quart Instant Pot, your insert pot will be full. This is a thick, satisfying Italian soup with lots of rich tomato flavor and bell pepper pizzazz. The herbs and broth add to the healthfulness of the soup. Cauliflower rice is an easy and perfect sub for the traditionally used white rice. Use whatever ground meat you like best or have on hand, or a combination. Ground beef is the most traditional choice. One more note on this soup: You can use frozen organic sliced bell peppers and frozen organic cauliflower rice if you wish, to make this soup super fast to assemble. You can use fresh if you prefer. I give both options below. It is no less rich and delicious from using frozen vegetables and the Instant Pot. Need it extra-extra fast and easy? Look for frozen pearl onions, and use them in place of chopping fresh ones. I very occasionally use this time saver crutch and haven't regretted it when I needed the help. These conveniences/compromises make soups like this one perfect for nights when we're extra tired or busy or getting home late but we want to feed our families nourishing food.

Serves 6 to 8.

INGREDIENTS:

2 pounds ground meat of choice: beef, lamb, pork, buffalo, wild game or turkey

6 cups bone broth

2 large onions or 6 small, diced (for Keto, replace the onions with green onions or fennel)

4 bell peppers, sliced and cut into bite-size pieces or 3 10-ounce packages frozen bell pepper slices

3 cups cauliflower rice, fresh or frozen

2 7-ounce jars tomato paste

3 tablespoons butter, or preferred fat

4 teaspoons sea salt, divided use

2 teaspoons dried basil

2 teaspoons dried oregano

1 teaspoon onion powder

1/2 teaspoon white pepper

INSTRUCTIONS:

1. Heat a large, deep skillet over medium-high heat. Add ground meat and 2 teaspoons sea salt. (If using a low-fat meat like wild game or turkey, add 2 tablespoons butter, ghee or non-dairy fat of choice.) Cook 5 minutes, breaking up meat in the pan with spatula.

2. Add onion powder and white pepper. Sauté an additional 5 minutes until mostly cooked through.

3. Remove ground meat to a large stock pot. Set aside.

4. Add 2 tablespoons butter or fat of choice to pan. Add onions and 1 teaspoon sea salt. Sauté 5 minutes, stirring regularly.

5. Add dried basil and oregano. Sauté another 5 minutes.

6. Transfer cooked onions and any cooking juices to large stock pot. Add bone broth, peppers, cauliflower rice, tomato paste and 1 teaspoon sea salt. Heat soup over medium-high heat, stirring occasionally, until it begins to simmer.

7. Cover, reduce heat and simmer slowly 35 to 40 minutes.

8. Stir and taste. Add 1/2 teaspoon sea salt, if needed. Serve.

INSTANT POT INSTRUCTIONS:

1. Press "Sauté" button on Instant Pot. Add ground meat and 2 teaspoons sea salt. (If using a low-fat meat like wild game or turkey, add 2 tablespoons butter, ghee or non-dairy fat of choice.) Cook 5 minutes, breaking up meat in the pot with a spatula.

2. Add onion powder and white pepper. Sauté an additional 5 minutes until mostly cooked through.

3. Remove ground beef to a bowl. Set aside.

4. Add 2 tablespoons butter or fat of choice to pot. Add onions and 1 teaspoon sea salt. Sauté 5 minutes, stirring regularly.

5. Add dried basil and oregano. Sauté another 5 minutes.

6. Add bone broth, peppers, cauliflower rice, tomato paste, 1 additional teaspoon of sea salt and cooked meat. Close and seal lid. Press "Soup" button. Decrease time using the "-" button to 15 minutes. When timer goes off, allow pressure to release naturally for 35 minutes. Carefully release remaining steam by opening steam vent.

7. Stir and taste. Add additional 1/2 teaspoon sea salt, if needed. Serve.

Shrimp Ceviche (Chilled)

Paleo, GAPS, Keto

Serve this salad-meets-soup with spoons and lime wedges.

Serves 4.

INGREDIENTS:

1 pound baby shrimp

8 ounces padron peppers

1 cucumber, diced

1 pound yellow and red tomatoes, any size, diced

1 cup shrimp stock, chilled (see Recipe Notes)

1/2 cup purple onion, diced

1/2 cup fresh cilantro, minced

1 lime, cut in wedges

Garnishes: extra-virgin olive oil, for drizzling, avocado and papaya (optional)

INSTRUCTIONS:

1. Preheat oven to 400 degrees Fahrenheit.

2. Place padron peppers on baking sheet. Bake 10 minutes.

3. Turn oven to broil and cook peppers until blackened somewhat on top side. Remove and set aside to cool.

4. In large bowl, combine shrimp, cucumber, tomatoes, onion and cilantro.

5. Pull stems out of padron peppers, and chop roughly. Add peppers and shrimp stock to ceviche. Stir again.

6. Serve with lime wedges, avocado and papaya on the side.

RECIPE NOTES:

Serving bowls may be nested in crushed ice. This soup makes a fun appetizer, too, served in small dishes.
See Shrimp Shell Stock recipe on Page 139.

Potato-Zucchini Soup With Dill

Paleo, phasing off GAPS

I have a lot of growing bodies in our home, so I serve this soup with a side of roasted chicken drumsticks. It's a good and economical way to add protein, but still allow the soup to be its own pure, vegetable-herb theme. A word about dill: While many reserve dill for making pickles or baking salmon, it's actually a fresh herb that sometimes deserves center stage. This soup features dill as the main flavor, and it's lovely. When hot, the soup is great plain, as mentioned above, but you can also poach a delicate white fish in the soup, beautiful with dill. When chilled, which is a variation discussed below the recipe, top the soup with baby shrimp, cooked crab or sautéed prawns. Dill is high in many vitamins and minerals and even has myriad health benefits.

Serves 4.

INGREDIENTS:

2 pounds Yukon Gold potatoes, cut in half, unpeeled

4 zucchini, sliced somewhat thickly into
3/4-inch rounds

1 large yellow onion, or 2 small, sliced

4 cups bone broth

2 tablespoons fat of choice, melted: lard, bacon fat, ghee

1-1/2 teaspoons sea salt, divided use

several sprigs fresh dill, about 3/4 ounce or
1 cup loosely packed sprigs

freshly ground black pepper, to taste

INSTRUCTIONS:

1. Preheat oven to 375 degrees Fahrenheit.

2. Place potatoes in a large saucepan and just cover with water. Add 1 teaspoon sea salt. Turn heat to high and bring water to a simmer. Reduce heat so potatoes slowly simmer. Cook about 45 minutes, until potatoes are tender to the center when poked with a knife.

3. While potatoes cook, place zucchini and onion on large baking tray. Add melted fat and 1/2 teaspoon sea salt. Stir to coat. Bake in preheated oven 45 minutes, until caramelized.

4. When potatoes are done, remove from heat and set aside to cool. Do not discard cooking water.

5. When zucchini is done, remove from oven. Allow to cool 30 minutes.

6. Place zucchini, onions, 3 cups bone broth and 3/4 cup dill in blender. Purée on medium speed 30 seconds, until smooth.

7. Pour zucchini purée into a large saucepan.

8. Refill blender with half the potatoes, and 3 cups liquid: the remaining cooking water from the potatoes, and make up the difference with bone broth. Purée on medium speed only 15 to 20 seconds, until mostly smooth. Do not over-blend potatoes.

9. Pour potato purée into large saucepan.

10. Rub peel from remaining potatoes. Dice potatoes and add to large saucepan.

11. Stir soup in large saucepan, and taste for salt and pepper. Adjust seasoning as needed. Reheat, top with fresh dill and serve.

12. Optional additional toppings: butter or ghee, chopped bacon, chopped fresh chives or green onions.

VARIATION:

If you wish, this soup can be served chilled during the hotter months. Make these modifications: Use avocado oil or olive oil to roast the zucchini. Make sure the bone broth has any fat skimmed off. Use a bone broth with less gelatin that is not solid when chilled. Chill finished soup, and serve cold.

Winter Squash Stew
With Chinese Five-Spice, Pork and Kale

Paleo, GAPS+, AIP+

This recipe can be doubled. It keeps well. Leftovers are good. And this soup can be a great way to use a lot of winter squash if you have a big harvest or find a great price on bulk squash. The soup is also naturally a bit sweet and well-liked by most, so kid-friendly. I list pork as the ground meat used, but it's good with other ground meat, as well — especially lamb.

Serves 4.

INGREDIENTS:

2-1/2 pounds butternut squash, baked (see Recipe Notes)
2 cups bone broth (and more if preferred)
1 pound ground pork

6 to 10 ounces kale, ribs separated and diced and leaves chopped

2 tablespoons fat of choice

1 tablespoon Chinese five-spice (for AIP, replace with 1 teaspoon cinnamon + 1 teaspoon ginger; for GAPS, replace with 1 teaspoon cinnamon, 1 teaspoon ginger, 1 teaspoon ground fennel seed and/or 1/4 teaspoon white pepper)

1-1/2 teaspoons sea salt, divided use, plus more to taste

INSTRUCTIONS:

1. Heat a large Dutch oven or pot over medium-high heat. Add fat, meat, kale ribs (no leaves yet) and sea salt. Sauté 10 to 12 minutes, breaking up meat in the pan as it cooks.

2. Add kale leaves and Chinese five-spice (or AIP/GAPS-legal spices). Sauté 2 minutes more.

3. While meat is cooking, place 2 cups broth and all the winter squash flesh from around the seed cavity into the blender. Purée until smooth.

4. Cube the remaining winter squash.

5. Add squash purée and squash cubes into pot. Stir and taste. Add more sea salt or broth if needed.

6. Heat and serve.

RECIPE NOTES:

See How to Bake Winter Squash on Page 149.

Gado-Gado Composed Stew With Peanut Butter Sauce

Paleo+, GAPS

Traditionally, gado-gado is an Indonesian salad with peanut dressing. This version sautés the same veggies (cabbage, radishes, cucumber and bean sprouts) and serves them with ladles of the hot stew base, a delicious peanut butter gravy, all topped with traditional hard-boiled eggs, garnished with lime, and served with a pitcher of hot broth. This is a fun GAPS diet dinner, and it doesn't contain any meat, which is nice for variety and the budget. Protein comes from the peanut butter (or Paleo nut or seed butter) and eggs.

Serves 4.

INGREDIENTS:

For Stew Base:

1 cup broth

2/3 cup peanut butter (sub another nut or seed butter for Paleo)

1 tablespoon tamarind paste

1 tablespoon fish sauce

1 tablespoon coconut amino acids

2 teaspoon honey

1 clove garlic, minced or crushed

1 drop lemongrass essential oil, optional

For Vegetable Sauté:

1 large head cabbage, finely shredded

2 to 3 cups bean sprouts

1 bunch radishes, sliced

1 cucumber, peeled and seeded and sliced

3 tablespoons fat of choice, for sautéing

1 teaspoon sea salt

Garnishes: fresh lime wedges, fresh cilantro, hard-boiled eggs, halved or quartered, 4 cups broth

INSTRUCTIONS:

1. Place all stew base ingredients in blender. Blend until smooth and creamy, stopping to scrape down sides of blender as needed — about 30 seconds total.

2. Pour stew base into a medium-size saucepan. Heat, stirring, over medium heat until hot through. Do not simmer. Keep warm on lowest stove top setting.

3. Heat large sauté pan over high heat. When hot, add fat, cabbage and sea salt. Sauté over medium-high heat for 10 minutes, stirring occasionally.

4. Add radishes and cook an additional 2 to 3 minutes.

5. Add bean sprouts and cucumbers, sautéing and stirring until heated through, an additional minute.

6. Serve sautéed vegetables in shallow bowls. Pour stew base over veggies. Add eggs, cilantro and lime wedges.

7. Place pitcher of hot broth on table to pour broth to the side and under veggies, or provide mugs for drinking broth on the side (both taste great). Provide forks and spoons for enjoying the meal.

Sprouted Lentil and Ham Hock Soup With Onions, Apples and Fennel

(with Instant Pot version) GAPS

Sprouted lentils cook very quickly — in just a few minutes! — and are much easier to digest, even than soaked beans. If you haven't tried sprouted lentils before, they come already sprouted, prepackaged and make bean soup edible for many who can't otherwise digest beans. Ham hocks are a favorite food from my childhood. My mom made great bean soups with ham hocks, but the meat was so good that it seemed there was never enough. Therefore, if you have meat lovers in your home, know that ham hocks have a big bone in the middle, so they're not all meat. You may need to use double what the recipe calls for if you want a really meaty soup. I tend to be a bit frugal because we already go through so much meat each day, so I stick with two ham hocks for this recipe. This soup thickens the second day. It has a bit of broth, as seen in the photos, if served the day it's made. But it gets quite a bit thicker and more stew-like if refrigerated overnight and reheated, which is a great way to make a meal ahead of time.

Serves 6.

INGREDIENTS:

10 cups water, divided use
2 cups packaged, dried, sprouted lentils (see Recipe Notes)
2 ham hocks
1-1/2 large or 3 small onions, diced
2 apples, diced
2 fennel bulbs, diced
2 tablespoons dried tarragon
2 teaspoons sea salt

INSTRUCTIONS:

1. Place 4 cups water, ham hocks, onions, apples, fennel, tarragon and sea salt in large stock pot. Bring to a boil. Reduce heat to medium-low, cover and simmer 2 hours.

2. While ham hocks cook, place beans in a medium-size saucepan with remaining 6 cups water. Bring to a boil. Reduce heat and simmer 5 minutes.

3. Remove from heat. Cover and let stand 5 minutes.

4. Pour beans through a colander to drain the remaining water.

5. When ham hocks are done cooking, remove them using tongs. Allow to cool slightly. Chop meat into bite-size pieces. (Compost or discard bones.)

6. Return meat to large pot with stock, apples, onions and fennel. Add beans. Stir and taste. Serve.

INSTANT POT INSTRUCTIONS:

1. Place 4 cups water, ham hocks, onions, apples, fennel, tarragon and sea salt into Instant Pot. Cover and seal. Shut steam valve. Press "Stew" button and increase time with the "+" button to 75 minutes.

2. When timer goes off, allow pressure to naturally release for 60 minutes. Press "Cancel" button. Carefully open steam vent using a hot pad or dish towel.

3. While the ham hocks and vegetables cook, place beans in a medium-size saucepan with remaining 6 cups water. Bring to a boil. Reduce heat and simmer 5 minutes.

4. Pour beans through a colander to drain the remaining water.

5. When ham hocks are done cooking, remove them using tongs. Allow to cool slightly. Chop meat into bite-size pieces. (Compost or discard bones.)

6. Return meat to Instant Pot with stock, apples, onions and fennel. Add beans. Stir and taste. Serve.

RECIPE NOTES:

See Resource Guide for a link to dried, sprouted lentils, Page 162.

Miso Soup

Paleo, Keto

Soy has gotten a bad rap among Traditional and Paleo health food advocates. It's hormone-altering and suppresses thyroid function. What many health foodies don't know is that soy can lose those negative effects when it is fermented. In fact, soy gains healing properties, little discussed, through fermentation. Miso is one such food, a fermented soybean paste that's delicious in soups and marinades. The reason miso should be invited into many more Traditional and Paleo homes is because of its anti-radiation and gut-healing effects. Miso has been studied both historically and scientifically. It regulates intestinal functions, relieves fatigue, aids digestion, can help to prevent colon cancer and ulcers, and also positively affects many other health issues including cancer, cholesterol and blood pressure issues. Some people should still avoid fermented soy and miso. Even fermented soy can be estrogenic for sensitive individuals. Be your best judge if miso is right for your body, or consult your doctor.

Serves 4.

INGREDIENTS:

6 cups broth or stock
1/2 cup fermented miso paste (see Recipe Notes)
1 pound daikon radish, peeled and cut into 1/2-inch cubes
1 bunch green onions, just the green ends, sliced thinly
3/4 to 1 ounce dried wakame

INSTRUCTIONS:

1. Place broth in a medium-large pot. Bring to a simmer over high heat.
2. Add daikon radish, reduce heat to medium and simmer 5 minutes.
3. While daikon cooks, place wakame in small bowl and soak in cool water for 10 minutes.
4. Add miso paste to broth. Whisk until dissolved. Turn off heat.
5. Place green onions and wakame in individual serving bowls, distributed evenly.
6. Add hot broth to each bowl and serve.

RECIPE NOTES:

See Resource Guide for a link to Shiro Miso fermented miso paste, Page 162.

Mexican Pork and Green Bean Stew

(an Instant Pot recipe) Paleo

Serves 6.

INGREDIENTS:

2 pounds country style ribs, or pork stew meat cut into 2-inch cubes

2 pounds fresh green beans, cut or snapped into 3-inch lengths (or see vegetable Variation below)

2 cups water + 1/4 cup additional water

2 tablespoons onion powder

2 tablespoons tapioca flour

1 tablespoon paprika

1 tablespoon oregano

2-1/4 teaspoons sea salt

1 teaspoon cumin

1/2 teaspoon freshly ground pepper

INSTRUCTIONS:

1. Place water and pork into Instant Pot. Sprinkle evenly with sea salt and then pepper. Top evenly with all herbs and spices. Attach lid and choose "Meat/Stew" button. Press "+" button to increase time to 45 minutes. Close steam valve.

2. When time has elapsed, allow pressure to release naturally for 1 hour.

3. Press "Cancel" button. Use hot pads or a dish towel to carefully open steam valve. Open lid. Use large slotted spoon to remove meat to a medium-size bowl. Set aside.

4. Combine remaining 1/4 cup water and tapioca flour in small bowl.

5. Press "Sauté" button on Instant Pot base. When soup broth begins to simmer, stir tapioca water well, then pour in all at once. Stir broth while it simmers until you see it thicken slightly.

6. Add green beans and simmer 5 minutes, stirring occasionally.

7. Press "Cancel" button twice to start the "Keep Warm" setting.

8. Place lid on green beans. They will continue to simmer 5 additional minutes while the Instant Pot base cools down.

9. Return meat to pot. Gently stir.

10. Serve or allow it to stay warm until ready to serve.

VARIATION:

If summer green beans are not in season, substitute them with an in-season vegetable that you have on hand: florets of cauliflower, collard greens, already cooked potato or white sweet potato.

RECIPE NOTES:

If your green beans are particularly young, tender and small, reduce their cooking time. Allow to simmer using "Sauté" button just 2 initial minutes, then press "Cancel" button.

Easy Basil-Pea Soup

Paleo, GAPS

This recipe is helpful for busy nights, making use of frozen peas and already-made broth.

Serves 3.

INGREDIENTS:

3 to 4 cups meat stock or bone broth (depending on how thick you want your soup)

1 bag organic frozen peas, 10 ounces

1 bag or box frozen pearl onions, 10 ounces or two onions, diced

1/2 cup fresh basil leaves

2 tablespoons extra-virgin olive oil, ghee, butter or bacon fat

1/4 teaspoon sea salt

freshly ground pepper, to taste

Optional: 1 to 2 drops basil essential oil (see Recipe Notes)

INSTRUCTIONS:

1. Place broth in a medium-large saucepan. Bring to a boil over medium-high heat.

2. Add onions. Cover and simmer 15 minutes over medium-low heat, until tender.

3. Add peas. Once broth returns to a simmer, remove from the heat. Allow to cool slightly.

4. Use handheld colander spoon or slotted spoon to scoop solids into blender (see Recipe Notes). Add enough broth to blend, about 2 to 3 cups. Add fresh basil, olive oil, sea salt and optional basil essential oil. Use caution when blending. Purée on low speed to start, and gradually increase speed to medium high until purée is smooth, about 1 minute.

5. Return purée to pot and heat over medium-high heat until hot-serving temperature. Add additional 1 cup broth if you want to thin the soup. Do not simmer.

6. Serve, garnished with optional freshly ground pepper.

RECIPE NOTES:

For GAPS/Primal, serve topped with a spoonful of probiotic sour cream.

See Resource Guide for a link to my recommended colander spoon, Page 161.

See Resource Guide for basil essential oil, Page 162.

Pumpkin- or Parsnip-Tahini Bisque With Turmeric, Ginger and Onions

Paleo, GAPS, VAD

I must adore hummus and tahini, because although we never eat hummus, I have a handful of soups and stews I make that borrow the flavors and texture of hummus by using tahini and certain spices in a stew. This stew is great to serve with roasted turkey or chicken, because you can dip bites of the meat into the stew, almost like a condiment. Meatballs would also work well here. And you can certainly add a riced vegetable (or organic white Basmati rice for VAD and gluten-free) to stretch the meal further. Parsnips are deliciously starchy and work great in the base of this thick stew — and most kinds of winter squash work great, too, for the GAPS version.

Serves 4.

INGREDIENTS:

7 to 8 cups parsnips, chopped and steamed until fork-tender (about 3 large parsnips) or winter squash for GAPS

3 cups broth, divided use

1 onion, diced

1/3 cup tahini

1/4 cup coconut oil, olive oil, butter or ghee, if tolerated (or a combination), divided use

2-inch piece fresh ginger

1 teaspoon turmeric

1/2 teaspoon sea salt

Garnish: toasted sesame oil (optional)

INSTRUCTIONS:

1. Heat small skillet over medium heat. Add 1 tablespoon fat of choice, diced onions and sea salt. Sauté onions 5 to 8 minutes, until beginning to brown.

2. Add 1/2 cup broth. Deglaze the pan. Simmer the onions 5 to 8 additional minutes until softened.

3. While onions cook, place the cooked parsnips and remaining 2-1/2 cups broth into blender. Add tahini, remaining 3 tablespoons fat, fresh ginger and turmeric. Purée on medium speed until smooth.

4. Using a spatula, pour the parsnip purée into a large saucepan. Heat gently, stirring over medium heat until hot.

5. Serve stew topped with a drizzle of toasted sesame oil, sautéed onions and a side of meat or optional rice.

Find recipes and insights at my blog, EAT BEAUTIFUL *(www.eatbeautiful.net), and Pinterest account (https://www. pinterest.com/ eatbeautifulnet/).*

Golden Macadamia Stew
With Chicken Satay Skewers

Paleo, GAPS, VAD

Serves 4 to 6.

INGREDIENTS:

For Chicken Skewers:

8 boneless, skinless chicken thighs, cut into 6 pieces each

3/4 cup sprouted nut butter (VAD-legal) (see Recipe Notes)

3/4 cup coconut cream, warmed and liquid — or if dairy is tolerated: fully cultured sour cream (for GAPS) or heavy cream, divided use (use 1/4 cup hulled tahini + 1/2 cup water for VAD)

1/2 cup white onion, roughly chopped

2-inch piece fresh ginger, roughly chopped

3 cloves garlic, roughly chopped

2 tablespoons sesame oil

1 teaspoon turmeric

1 teaspoon sea salt

1/4 teaspoon cinnamon

For Macadamia Stew:

1 large head cauliflower, roughly chopped (use peeled white russet potato, diced, for VAD)

3 cups flavorful bone broth or meat stock, slightly warm or room temperature

8 ounces macadamia nuts, preferably raw and unsalted, soaked for 2 hours or overnight

2 tablespoons coconut oil (or butter or ghee, if tolerated)

2 cloves garlic, minced or crushed

1 teaspoon sea salt

1/2 teaspoon onion powder

Garnishes: satay sauce, chopped raisins, chopped nuts

INSTRUCTIONS:

1. Soak 9 wooden skewers (8 to 10 inches long) in warm water for 15 to 20 minutes.

2. Pour soaked macadamia nuts into colander over sink and rinse well.

3. Place macadamia nuts and 2 cups broth in blender. Purée on medium-high speed until mostly smooth, about 45 seconds.

For Chicken Skewers:

1. Place all chicken skewer ingredients, except chicken and reserved 1/4 cup cream, in food processor (or high-powered blender). Pulse until well mixed and a somewhat smooth paste is formed. This is the satay sauce and the chicken marinade.

2. Pour 1 cup sauce into large bowl. Reserve the remaining satay sauce in smaller bowl. Add chicken to large bowl and stir to coat. Marinate 2 to 4 hours or overnight if preferred.

3. Preheat oven to 400 degrees. Place the chicken on prepared skewers, leaving about 1-1/2 inches free on each end.

4. Line a baking sheet with parchment paper. Line up skewers on the baking sheet.

5. Bake 20 to 25 minutes, until chicken is tinged with brown and cooked through.

For Macadamia Stew:

1. Place remaining 1 cup broth in medium saucepan. Add cauliflower (or diced potato) and garlic. Cover and cook 10 minutes over medium heat, until soft and cooked through.

2. Transfer to blender. Add coconut oil and onion powder. Purée.

3. Pour macadamia purée into a large saucepan. Add cauliflower purée and sea salt. Heat over medium heat to a slow simmer, stirring regularly.

4. In a separate small saucepan, gently heat remaining satay sauce and remaining 1/4 cup cream.

5. To serve, ladle stew into bowls. Drizzle satay sauce over the top. Top each stew with Chicken Satay Skewers. Garnish with chopped raisins and/or chopped macadamia nuts.

RECIPE NOTES:

See VAD-legal grocery list at https://eatbeautiful.net/VAD_grocery .

Hearty Chili
With Mushrooms and Red Bell Peppers

(with Instant Pot variation) Paleo, GAPS, Keto {A "Dump and Cook" Recipe}

Chili made with stew meat is naturally high in fat and delicious for those who love chunks of tender meat and want to change up the frequent use of ground meat. As with most chili recipes, choose from beef, pork, lamb, venison, elk, etc. (Do not use low-fat meats such as turkey.) You'll love the flavorful "gravy" base of this chili, full of great ingredients and classic, comforting flavors.

Serves 4 to 6.

INGREDIENTS:

2 pounds stew meat

2 cups bone broth (and more as needed for stovetop version)

7 ounces tomato paste

2 red bell peppers, sliced

1 pound mushrooms of choice, stems removed and mushrooms quartered

3 tablespoons traditional fat of choice, divided use (Optional: Use the extra 1 tablespoon of fat if your stew meat is lean. If your stew meat has lots of fat and fatty edges, you won't need it.)

2 tablespoons cocoa powder

1 tablespoon chili powder

1 tablespoon cumin

1 tablespoon dried oregano

5 cloves garlic, crushed or minced

2-1/2 teaspoons sea salt, divided use

2 teaspoons dried thyme

1/2 teaspoon white pepper

Garnishes: fresh cilantro and probiotic sour cream (optional)

INSTRUCTIONS:

1. To large Dutch oven with tight-fitting lid or large stock pot with lid, add stew meat, bone broth, tomato paste, mushrooms, 1 tablespoon fat if meat is lean, cocoa powder, chili powder, cumin, oregano, garlic, 2 teaspoons sea salt, thyme and white pepper. Heat pan over medium-high heat as you stir to mix well.

2. Reduce heat and cover. Slowly simmer 2 hours, stirring occasionally. Add more broth if needed as liquid evaporates.

3. While chili slow cooks, heat remaining 2 tablespoons fat in large cast-iron skillet over medium-high heat. Add red bell pepper slices and final 1/2 teaspoon sea salt. Sauté 5 to 8 minutes, until peppers are wilted and browned in places. Set aside.

4. When chili cooking time has elapsed, stir in red bell peppers.

5. Serve, garnished with optional fresh cilantro and probiotic sour cream.

INSTANT POT INSTRUCTIONS:

1. To Instant Pot, add stew meat, bone broth, tomato paste, mushrooms, 1 tablespoon fat if meat is lean, cocoa powder, chili powder, cumin, oregano, garlic, 2 teaspoons sea salt, thyme and white pepper. Stir to mix well. Attach Instant Pot lid. Close steam valve. Press "Stew" button and press "+" button to 90 minutes.

2. When timer goes off, allow pressure to release naturally for 30 minutes. Place dish towel or hot pad over steam vent. Press "Cancel" button and carefully open steam valve to release remaining pressure.

3. While chili pressure cooks, heat remaining 2 tablespoons fat in large cast-iron skillet over medium-high heat. Add red bell pepper slices and final 1/2 teaspoon sea salt. Sauté 5 to 8 minutes, until peppers are wilted and browned in places. Set aside.

4. When chili cooking time has elapsed, and lid is removed, stir in red bell peppers.

5. Serve, garnished with optional fresh cilantro and probiotic sour cream.

Chinese Sesame Chicken

(with Instant Pot variation) Paleo, GAPS, Keto, VAD

This soup provides the basic template for a creamy (but dairy-free) base with wonderful, well-loved Chinese flavors. The ingredients are very simple, but you can easily add one other veggie to make the meal bigger or to add more interest or nutrition: For Paleo, cubes of already cooked sweet potatoes. For GAPS, cubes of already cooked butternut squash. For Keto, cooked cauliflower rice. For VAD, white basmati rice. Steamed greens may also be stirred in for most diets, not VAD. Or keep it as simple as it is below.

Serves 4.

INGREDIENTS:

6 cups water

1-1/2 pounds chicken thighs, bone in, skin on

3 cups cauliflower rice, cooked — or 2 cups cauliflower rice + 1 cup cooked winter squash, sweet potato or baked onion (not Keto or VAD) (use 3 cups cooked, chopped white potatoes or parsnips for VAD)

1-1/2 cups shiitake mushrooms

1 tablespoon sea salt + 3/4 teaspoon, divided use

1/2 cup sesame tahini, hulled

1/4 cup toasted sesame oil

1/4 cup fresh ginger, minced small (no need to peel it first)

2 tablespoons avocado oil

3 cloves garlic, minced or crushed

INSTRUCTIONS:

1. Place water, chicken and 1 tablespoon sea salt in large saucepan or stock pot. Heat over medium-high heat until water begins to boil. Skim off any scum. Reduce heat to medium low. Simmer 30 minutes.

2. Remove chicken with slotted spoon to plate to cool slightly.

3. Heat large Dutch oven or saucepan over medium-high heat. Add fat of choice, mushrooms and remaining sea salt. Sauté 5 minutes.

4. Reduce heat to low. Add ginger and garlic and stir 1 minute more.

5. Remove skin from chicken and place in blender. Add to blender: cauliflower rice, tahini, sesame oil and 3 cups broth. Purée until smooth and creamy, about 45 seconds. If using potatoes for VAD, blend just 20 to 25 seconds.

6. Pour purée into Dutch oven or saucepan with mushrooms. Begin to heat over medium-low heat.

7. Remove chicken from bones. Chop chicken into bite-size pieces. Add to heating pot and stir.

8. Taste and add a bit more broth if desired. Serve.

INSTANT POT INSTRUCTIONS:

1. Place water, chicken and 1 tablespoon sea salt in Instant Pot. Attach lid, close steam valve and press "Soup" button.

2. When timer goes off, allow pressure to release naturally for 30 minutes, then press "Cancel" button and carefully quick release remaining pressure.

3. Remove chicken with slotted spoon to plate to cool slightly.

4. Pour meat stock into large storage container.

5. Return insert pot to Instant Pot base. Press "Sauté" button on Instant Pot. Add fat of choice, mushrooms and remaining sea salt. Sauté 5 minutes.

6. Press "Cancel" button. Add ginger and garlic and stir 1 minute more, as the Instant Pot's heat cools gradually.

7. Remove skin from chicken and place in blender. Add to blender: cauliflower rice, tahini, sesame oil and 3 cups broth from storage container. Purée until smooth and creamy, about 45 seconds. If using potatoes for VAD, blend just 20 to 25 seconds.

8. Pour purée into Instant Pot with mushrooms. Press "Sauté" button again to briefly reheat. Stir occasionally. If soup gets too hot, press "Cancel" button twice so IP switches to "Keep Warm" setting.

9. Remove chicken from bones. Chop chicken into bite-size pieces. Add to heating pot and stir.

10. Taste and add a bit more broth if desired. Serve.

Gumbo

Paleo, GAPS, Keto

Gumbo is a simple dish to prepare, with fiery spice for the fun of it. Gumbo is Southern comfort food that originated in Louisiana, created by Africans. While this stew uses sausages and shrimp, gumbo proteins vary considerably: crab, oysters, turkey, squirrel, rabbit, beef, ham, chicken, bacon, duck, hard-boiled eggs and quail eggs. I've given a range below for the amount of shrimp and sausage used in this recipe, as pre-packaged shrimp and sausages vary in quantity.

Serves 4 to 6.

INGREDIENTS:

12 to 16 ounces frozen large shrimp, deveined

12 to 16 ounces sausage, cut into rounds

2 cups bone broth

1 bell pepper, diced

1 onion, diced

2 celery stalks, diced

15 ounces diced tomatoes, canned or jarred (see Recipe Notes)

1 bag frozen okra, or 1/2 pound fresh okra, cut into rounds (optional, omit for GAPS)

6 to 7 ounces tomato paste

2 tablespoons fat of choice

4 cloves garlic, minced or crushed

1 tablespoon Cajun seasoning (see Recipe Notes)

1 teaspoon sea salt

1/2 teaspoon thyme

1/2 teaspoon oregano

1/2 teaspoon pepper

1/8 teaspoon cayenne pepper (optional)

Garnish: fresh parsley, chopped (optional)

INSTRUCTIONS:

1. Heat large skillet over high heat. Add fat, onions, peppers, celery and sea salt. Sauté 8 to 10 minutes, reducing the heat to medium after the first 5 minutes, until vegetables are well-wilted and beginning to brown.

2. Add Cajun spices, thyme, oregano and pepper. Stir and cook 2 minutes, until fragrant.

3. Add broth, tomatoes, okra, tomato paste and garlic. Bring to a simmer. Cook 10 minutes.

4. Add shrimp and sausage. Cook 3 to 5 minutes, stirring, until shrimp is cooked through.

5. Serve, topped with fresh parsley.

RECIPE NOTES:

See Resource Guide for links to my Cajun seasoning and jarred tomatoes recommendation, Page 162.

Easy Cabbage Roll Soup

Paleo, GAPS, Keto

Serves 4 to 6.

INGREDIENTS:

6 cups cabbage, thinly sliced, then chopped so the pieces aren't too long

4 cups bone broth or meat stock

28 ounces stewed tomatoes

3 cups cauliflower rice, fresh or frozen

1 pound ground beef

1 onion, diced

7 ounces tomato paste

4 cloves garlic, minced or crushed

2 tablespoons olive oil

2 tablespoons dried parsley

1 tablespoon coconut sugar or honey, for GAPS

1-1/2 teaspoons sea salt

1 teaspoon dried thyme

Garnish: fresh parsley

INSTRUCTIONS:

1. Heat the olive oil in a large pot over medium-high heat.

2. Add the ground beef, onions, parsley, thyme and sea salt. Cook, breaking up the meat with a spatula, until the meat and onions are partially cooked and browned, about 5 minutes.

3. Add the tomatoes, breaking them up with a spatula if they're whole. Also add broth, cabbage, tomato paste, garlic and sweetener. Stir well. Bring to a simmer and cook 20 minutes, until cabbage is well-wilted.

4. Add cauliflower rice and bring to a simmer again. Cook 5 minutes more, stirring once or twice.

5. Serve, garnished with fresh parsley.

soups and stews
with dairy

CHAPTER FOUR

Soups and Stews With Dairy

The soups in this chapter are Primal
(the dairy-inclusive version of Paleo), GAPS, Keto and
sometimes include AIP+ and VAD recipes.

Broccoli White Cheddar Soup

Primal, GAPS, Keto

A classic cheese soup.

Serves 4 to 6.

INGREDIENTS:

6 cups fresh broccoli, cut into small pieces, or frozen, partially defrosted

4 cups bone broth, divided use

2 onions, diced

8 ounces sharp cheddar, or other aged cheese like Gruyere, cut into 1-inch cubes

1 cup cream

1 cup milk, preferably raw (use cream for Keto)

1/4 cup gelatin

1 tablespoon butter

1-1/2 teaspoons sea salt, divided use

1 teaspoon onion powder

2 cloves garlic, diced or minced

freshly ground black pepper, to taste

INSTRUCTIONS:

1. Steam fresh broccoli until bright green and tender, but not mushy, about 6 minutes. If using frozen, steam 2 minutes. Set aside.

2. Heat large saucepan. Add butter, onions and 1/2 teaspoon sea salt. Sauté onions 10 minutes.

3. After 10 minutes, stir in 3 cups broth and simmer 15 minutes.

4. Stir in garlic. Turn off heat, and allow to cool slightly.

5. While onions sauté, heat milk and cream in small saucepan, stirring occasionally, until steaming, but not so hot you can't put your finger into it.

6. While milk and cream are heating, add the following to blender: cheese cubes, onion powder and 1/2 teaspoon sea salt.

7. Add hot cream and milk to blender. Sprinkle gelatin over its surface. Blend about 15 seconds.

8. Pour back into small saucepan and keep warm over lowest heat.

9. Place 3 cups steamed broccoli into blender. Ladle about 3 cups warm onions and bone broth into blender. Add remaining 1/2 teaspoon sea salt. Purée until smooth.

10. Add purée to soup pot. Add remaining pieces of broccoli that were set aside. Add cheese sauce. Heat until hot, stirring often. Do not allow to simmer.

11. Serve.

Broccoli and Cheddar Buffalo Chicken Soup

(with Instant Pot version) Primal, GAPS, Keto

Serves 4.

INGREDIENTS:

1-1/2 pounds chicken thighs, boneless, skinless

7 ounces cheddar cheese, cut into about 1-inch cubes

4 cups water

1-1/2 cups heavy cream, preferably raw and not ultra-pasteurized

2 to 3 heads broccoli, about 4 cups chopped small (peeled and chopped stalks may be included)

1 tablespoon hot sauce or more, to taste, up to 3 tablespoons (see Recipe Notes)

2 tablespoons butter

1 tablespoon sea salt + 1/2 teaspoon, divided use

1 tablespoon gelatin

1-1/2 teaspoons onion powder

1 teaspoon garlic powder

INSTRUCTIONS:

1. Place the following ingredients in a large saucepan or Dutch oven: water, chicken thighs and 2 teaspoons sea salt. Simmer slowly, covered, over medium heat 15 minutes.

2. Turn off the heat, and allow to sit 10 additional minutes.

3. Remove chicken thighs with slotted spoon. Set them on a large plate to cool slightly. Set aside 2 cups meat stock (the water that's now flavorful and nutrient-dense) to cool slightly. Store remaining meat stock for another use, leaving saucepan empty.

4. While chicken cools, add 2 tablespoons butter to large cast-iron skillet. Once melted, add broccoli and 1 teaspoon sea salt. Cover, allowing broccoli to sauté and steam 5 minutes.

5. Remove lid, stir, and allow to cook an additional 5 minutes.

6. While broccoli cooks, add cheese and cream to blender. Top with slightly cooled stock, hot sauce, onion powder and garlic powder. Add gelatin and remaining 1/2 teaspoon sea salt. Purée 15 seconds on low speed and 15 seconds on medium speed.

7. Meanwhile, chop cooling chicken into bite-size pieces, about six to eight pieces per thigh. (Do not shred chicken.)

8. Return chicken and purée from blender to saucepan. Add broccoli. Heat over low heat, stirring regularly, until soup is hot. Do not allow to simmer.

9. Serve.

INSTANT POT INSTRUCTIONS:

1. Place the following into Instant Pot: water, chicken thighs and 2 teaspoons sea salt. Seal lid and close steam vent. Press "Chicken" button and "-" button to reduce cooking time to 10 minutes.

2. When cooking time has elapsed, do a quick pressure release by first pressing the "Cancel" button. Then place a dish towel over the steam vent and carefully open it. Take off lid.

3. Remove chicken thighs with slotted spoon. Set thighs on large plate to cool slightly. Also remove 2 cups meat stock (the water that's now flavorful and nutrient-dense) to cool slightly. Store remaining meat stock for another use, leaving Instant Pot empty.

4. While chicken cools, press "Sauté" button on Instant Pot. Add 2 tablespoons butter to Instant Pot. Once melted, add broccoli and 1 teaspoon sea salt. Place clear glass lid on Instant Pot, allowing broccoli to sauté and steam 5 minutes.

5. Remove lid, stir, and allow to cook an additional 5 minutes.

6. While broccoli cooks, add cheese and cream to blender. Top with slightly cooled broth, hot sauce, onion powder and garlic powder. Add gelatin and remaining 1/2 teaspoon sea salt. Purée 15 second on low speed and 15 seconds on medium speed.

7. Meanwhile chop cooling chicken into bite-size pieces, about 6 to 8 per thigh. (Do not shred chicken.)

8. Return chicken and purée from blender to Instant Pot with broccoli. Keep "Sauté" button on, and stir constantly but slowly, until soup is hot. Do not allow to bubble away or rapidly simmer. Press "Keep Warm/Cancel" button twice if the "Sauté" button gets too hot.

9. Serve.

RECIPE NOTES:

See Resource Guide for a link to my hot sauce recommendation, Page 162.

Chicken and Aged Cheddar Cauliflower Soup

Primal, GAPS, Keto

High in healthy fats, the combination of sour cream, aged cheddar, stock and a bit of extra gelatin creates a gut-healthy, creamy, smooth base for this soup that's also full of cauliflower's brassica nutrition and good protein.

Serves 4.

INGREDIENTS:

4 cups meat stock or bone broth (+ any chicken skin leftover from making stock)

3 cups leftover chicken, chopped

1 large head cauliflower, steamed until tender (see Recipe Notes)

7 ounces aged cheddar, roughly chopped into 1-inch cubes (I use one block of Kerrygold Aged Cheddar.)

8 ounces sour cream (fully cultured for GAPS)

1 tablespoon gelatin

1 teaspoon sea salt

3/4 teaspoon garlic powder

INSTRUCTIONS:

1. In large saucepan, heat stock or broth until very warm but not yet simmering.

2. Add 2 to 3 cups broth to the blender with the following: about 1/3 of the cooked cauliflower, half the cheddar, half the sour cream, half of the gelatin, all of the sea salt and garlic powder. Purée on low speed and then increase to medium-high speed, until purée is smooth, about 40 seconds.

3. Pour remaining hot broth from saucepan into a large dish or measuring bowl to briefly set aside, making room for the purée in the saucepan.

4. Pour purée into empty saucepan.

5. Pour remaining set aside broth into blender and add an additional 1/3 of the cauliflower, the remaining cheddar, sour cream and gelatin. Purée again on low speed and then increase to medium-high speed, until purée is smooth.

6. Pour all of the puréed soup into large saucepan. Add chicken.

7. Chop remaining cooked cauliflower into bite-size pieces. Add cauliflower to soup.

8. Heat soup over medium-high heat, stirring constantly, until piping hot. Do not allow to simmer or boil.

9. Ladle into bowls and serve, garnished with freshly ground black pepper, crispy bacon or fresh minced parsley, if desired.

VARIATION:

Fresh or frozen spinach may also be stirred into this hot soup before serving for a one-dish dinner, complete with leafy greens. Also, 1/4 teaspoon nutmeg is a nice addition with the spinach, and may also be grated on top for garnish.

RECIPE NOTES:

See How to Cook Cauliflower: Three Ways on Page 148.

Chicken Cordon Bleu Stew

Primal, GAPS, Keto

Serves 6.

INGREDIENTS:

1-1/2 pounds boneless skinless chicken thighs

1 large head of cauliflower, chopped into small pieces

1-1/2 cups heavy whipping cream, or use fully cultured sour cream for GAPS

6 cups water

5 ounces ham, cooked and diced (OK to use cooked, chopped bacon or cured prosciutto for GAPS)

4 ounces Gruyere, Swiss or aged cheddar cheese, grated

3 ounces blue cheese, crumbled

1 clove garlic

2 teaspoons sea salt

1 teaspoon dry mustard

freshly ground black pepper, to taste

fresh sage, optional

INSTRUCTIONS:

1. In large saucepan, heat water and sea salt over medium-high heat.

2. When water boils, reduce heat to medium. Add chicken and slow simmer 20 minutes.

3. Remove chicken with slotted spoon and set aside. When cool enough to handle, chop into small bite-size pieces.

4. Add cauliflower to chicken meat stock in saucepan. Slow simmer 8 minutes. Remove with slotted spoon and set aside to cool slightly.

5. Ladle 2 cups broth into blender. (Store remainder of meat stock in fridge for another use.)

6. Add to blender: 1 cup cooked cauliflower, garlic and mustard. Purée until smooth, about 30 seconds.

7. Pour purée into empty saucepan. Add cooked chicken, remaining cooked cauliflower, heavy cream, diced ham and gruyere. Turn stove heat to low. Stir until cheese melts, but do not allow soup to simmer.

8. Serve soup, garnished with blue cheese and black pepper. Optionally, add chopped fresh sage.

VARIATION:

For more leafy greens, add fresh chopped or frozen spinach with the cooked chicken and other ingredients. Allow to wilt and heat through. Serve with garnishes.

Find recipes and insights at my blog, EAT BEAUTIFUL *(www.eatbeautiful.net), and Pinterest account (https://www. pinterest.com/ eatbeautifulnet/).*

Butter Chicken

(with Instant Pot version) Paleo, GAPS, Keto

I simply love this dish and this sauce! When I open the lid on the finished dish, the texture of the sauce/broth woos me. It's thick, but there is no thickener. Rather the sauce is high-fat and rich with tomatoes, butter, spices and coconut cream. A meat stock is created during the cooking process. The sauce coats and bathes the tender chicken. I like to make this dish with no veggies in the main pot and then serve it with roasted cauliflower (see Roasted Cauliflower recipe on Page 148). It can also be served over cauliflower rice. If you are extra-pinched for time and using the Instant Pot version of this recipe, you can also throw in a bag or two of pre-cut winter squash cubes (for Paleo and GAPS) or cauliflower rice and spinach, and you'd have a complete meal when it's done cooking. Or roast a whole winter squash in the oven while the stew cooks. Stovetop or Instant Pot? This recipe turns out great both ways, and both are easy. If you choose the Instant Pot recipe, it is A "Dump and Cook" Recipe: Simply place all ingredients in the pot, cook, stir and serve.

Serves 4 to 6.

INGREDIENTS:

1-1/2 pounds skinless, boneless chicken thighs, cut into about 6 pieces each, or 3 pounds chicken drumsticks — skin on, bone-in (see Recipe Notes)

1 can full fat coconut milk or coconut cream

1 cup filtered water

1 large onion, diced (optional — omit for Keto or for faster assembly)

1 6- to 7-ounce jar tomato paste

2 tablespoons ghee or butter (OK to omit or use bacon fat or coconut oil if dairy-free)

5 cloves garlic, crushed or minced

2-inch piece ginger, grated or minced

2 teaspoons garam masala

1-1/2 teaspoons sea salt

1 teaspoon coriander

1 teaspoon cumin

1 teaspoon paprika

1 teaspoon turmeric

1/4 teaspoon black pepper (optional)

1/4 teaspoon white pepper (or red cayenne pepper if you want it spicy, optional)

INSTRUCTIONS:

1. Heat ghee over high heat in large cast-iron skillet or sauté pan with lid. Add onions and 1/2 teaspoon sea salt. Sauté 10 minutes.

2. Add chicken and spices: garam masala, coriander, cumin, paprika, turmeric and optional peppers. Cover and cook about 5 minutes.

3. Add tomato paste, coconut cream, water, garlic, ginger and sea salt. Stir, scraping up any bits that are sticking to the bottom of the pan. Cover and simmer over medium heat 10 minutes.

4. Using tongs or two forks, flip chicken pieces over. Cover and cook 10 additional minutes.

5. Stir and serve with roasted cauliflower (or keep warm over low heat until you're ready to serve).

INSTANT POT INSTRUCTIONS:

1. Place into Instant Pot: chicken, tomato paste, coconut cream, water, optional onion, butter, garlic, ginger, sea salt, garam masala, coriander, cumin, paprika, turmeric and optional peppers. Seal lid, making sure steam valve is closed, and press "Poultry" button. Timer will read, "15 minutes."

2. When timer goes off, allow pressure to release naturally 30 minutes. Press, "Cancel" button, open steam valve and remove lid.

3. If using chicken drumsticks, see directions below for removing skin, soft tissue and meat from bones.

4. Otherwise, stir and serve with a side of roasted cauliflower or cauliflower rice, to sop up all of the good sauce.

RECIPE NOTES:

What cut of chicken should you buy? If you want an easier and faster prep time, I recommend the thighs. If you vote less money and more GAPS-style healing, I recommend the drumsticks. If you choose the thighs, the recipe is very straightforward; just follow the instructions above.

If you choose the drumsticks, they are more cost-effective, and the bones and skin cook in the sauce and broth, adding nutrition and flavor. After cooking, separate out and allow the meat to cool slightly. Then remove the skin and any soft connective tissue. Place it in the blender with about 2 cups of the butter chicken sauce. Purée on medium speed about 30 seconds, until smooth. Add this purée back into the main cooking pot. Meanwhile remove all meat from bones. Add it back to the cooking pot, as well.

Cheeseburger Soup

Primal, GAPS, Keto

In this soup, gelatin plays a special role. Not only a gut-healthy ingredient, gelatin helps to stabilize the cheese sauce, creating a smooth-texture and family-friendly comfort food. This soup can be served simply, as is, with maybe just some grated cheese on top as a garnish. It can also be used as a fun soup for a serve-yourself buffet with lots of traditional low-carb cheeseburger toppings: fried eggs, blue cheese, bacon pieces, pickle slices, diced tomatoes and sautéed or grilled onions.

Serves 6 to 8.

INGREDIENTS:

For Cheese Sauce:

8 ounces sharp cheddar, or other aged cheese like Gruyere, cut into cubes

1-1/2 cups cream (use cultured cream for GAPS)

1/4 cup gelatin

1 teaspoon onion powder

1/2 teaspoon sea salt

For Meat and Veggie Soup Base:

2 pounds ground beef

3 whole tomatoes, diced or 2 cups stewed tomatoes, drained

2 bunches green onions, diced

3-1/2 cups bone broth, divided use

1 12-ounce package frozen cauliflower rice, defrosted — or use 3-1/2 cups homemade cauliflower rice, steamed

2 cloves garlic

1-1/2 teaspoons sea salt

Garnishes: more grated cheddar or-low carb cheeseburger toppings (optional)

INSTRUCTIONS:

For Cheese Sauce:

1. Heat cream in a small saucepan, stirring occasionally, until steaming, but not so hot you can't put your finger into it.

2. While cream is heating, add the following to blender: cheese cubes, onion powder and 1/2 teaspoon sea salt.

3. Add hot cream to blender. Sprinkle gelatin over its surface. Blend about 15 seconds.

4. Pour back into saucepan and keep warm over lowest heat.

For Meat and Veggie Soup Base:

1. Place ground beef and 1-1/2 teaspoons sea salt in large saucepan. Sauté over medium heat until most of the pink is gone, breaking meat into small pieces with spatula, about 10 minutes.

2. Add tomatoes, green onions and garlic. Sauté an additional 10 minutes.

3. Add 1-1/2 cups broth and heat almost to simmering, about 5 to 10 minutes.

4. Place cauliflower rice in blender. Add remaining 2 cups bone broth. Purée until smooth.

5. Add to large saucepan and stir well. Add Cheese Sauce, stirring again. Heat to hot without simmering, stirring often.

6. Serve, topped with optional additional grated cheese or low carb cheeseburger toppings.

Borscht

(an Instant Pot recipe) Paleo, GAPS, AIP+

Serves 8 to 10.

INGREDIENTS:

8 cups bone broth or meat stock

2 pounds ground beef

5 to 6 small beets, whole and unpeeled

2 pounds carrots, diced or shredded

1 small head cabbage, sliced thinly or shredded

1 large onion, diced

1 6- to 7-ounce jar tomato paste, optional (not AIP, OK to leave out if nightshade sensitivity)

2 tablespoons fresh lemon juice

2 tablespoons honey, maple syrup, coconut sugar OR a bit of stevia, to taste (not AIP)

1-2/3 tablespoons sea salt

2 teaspoons dried dill

freshly ground black pepper, to taste (not AIP)

Garnish: fresh dill (optional)

INSTRUCTIONS:

1. Add beets and 2 cups broth to Instant Pot. Seal lid, shut steam valve and press "Manual" and "-" to 10 minutes.

2. When time has elapsed, press "Cancel" button. Place dish towel over steam valve and release steam. Remove lid. Remove beets to cool slightly.

3. Press "Sauté" button on Instant Pot. To the broth in the Instant Pot, add onion, beef and sea salt. Using a large spatula, break up meat into small pieces as it cooks, until not much pink remains, 5 to 8 minutes.

4. Add carrots, cabbage and dill, stirring it into the meat somewhat. Place lid on and allow to simmer 10 minutes.

5. While vegetables cook, run beets under cool water. Skins will rub off easily. Once peeled, dice and set aside.

6. Remove lid of Instant Pot and stir vegetables and meat. Replace lid and simmer an additional 5 minutes. Press "Cancel" button twice, to turn on "Keep Warm" setting.

7. To Instant Pot, add beets, tomato paste, lemon juice and sweetener of choice. Stir well. Taste.

8. Serve with optional fresh dill and probiotic sour cream (not AIP).

Extra-Creamy Cream of Pumpkin Soup With Bacon Garnish

Paleo, GAPS, AIP+

Partially cooked bacon is puréed into the base of this soup, which adds flavor, depth and creaminess. This soup is also touched with great autumn herbs and your cream of choice (with dairy-free and cultured options).

Serves 6.

INGREDIENTS:

3 pounds winter squash, kabocha or butternut, already cooked, peeled and de-seeded (see Recipe Notes)

2 cups meat stock or bone broth

1 cup coconut cream (for AIP), heavy cream or sour cream (fully cultured for GAPS)

1/2 pound bacon, divided use

2 teaspoons dried sage, or 1/4 cup loosely packed fresh sage

1 teaspoon sea salt

1/2 teaspoon dried thyme or 2 tablespoons fresh leaves

1/2 teaspoon onion powder

INSTRUCTIONS:

1. Preheat oven to 400 degrees Fahrenheit.

2. Spread out bacon on baking tray. Bake 10 minutes. Remove 2 pieces and set them aside.

3. Return remaining bacon to oven to finish baking, another 5 to 8 minutes, depending on thickness of bacon. (Watch closely to prevent burning.)

4. Separate out 1/4 of the winter squash. Cut it into 1-inch cubes. Set aside.

5. Add the rest of the winter squash to the blender. Also add to the blender: broth, the 2 pieces of half-cooked bacon, sage, sea salt, thyme and onion powder. Purée about 30 seconds, until smooth.

6. Transfer to large saucepan. Stir in cream of choice and cubes of winter squash. Heat over medium-high heat, stirring, until steamy hot.

7. Chop or crumble fully cooked bacon on top of soup and serve.

VARIATION:

Dice and sauté two onions until browned and soft. Add and stir onions into soup with the cream and squash cubes.

RECIPE NOTES:

See How to Bake Winter Squash on Page 149.

Thai Chard Bisque

Paleo, GAPS, AIP+ Keto

Drinking bisque from a mug is a pleasure. Warming, nourishing and flavorful, you'll love this fresh ginger, leafy greens, high-fat treat. Full of veggies and broth, it makes a wonderful snack, light meal or side dish.

Serves 4 to 6.

INGREDIENTS:

4 cups bone broth or meat stock

3/4 pound cauliflower, trimmed of leaves and rough stem, cut into medium-size pieces

1 large bunch Swiss chard, about 7 to 8 cups chopped, stalks included

2 green onions, roughly chopped

2- to 4-inch piece fresh ginger, cut into smaller pieces

6 tablespoons unsalted butter (use coconut oil for AIP)

1/2 teaspoon sea salt

2 to 4 drops basil essential oil

INSTRUCTIONS:

1. Place 3 cups bone broth and cauliflower into saucepan. Bring to simmer over high heat. Reduce heat to medium, cover and simmer 10 minutes.

2. While cauliflower cooks add remaining ingredients to blender jar: 1 cup bone broth, chard, green onions, ginger (quantity based on taste preference), butter, sea salt and essential oil (start with 2 drops and add more if desired).

3. After 10 minutes remove bone broth and cauliflower from heat. Carefully ladle hot liquid and solids into blender.

4. Put on blender lid. Reduce speed to lowest setting.

5. Using caution when puréeing hot liquids, begin blending. Increase speed gradually to medium. Blend soup 35 to 50 seconds, until smooth.

6. Taste to adjust flavor to preference: add more ginger, sea salt or basil essential oil as needed. (I usually add 1/4 teaspoon additional sea salt and one more drop basil EO.) Once again on lowest setting, blend again briefly, if additions are made.

6. Serve by the mug. Garnish with thinly sliced green onions if desired.

Indian Spinach Stew With Cheese Cubes (Palaak Paneer Variation)

Primal, GAPS, Keto

Usually Palaak Paneer is a spicy dish made with green chilies. I've omitted the chilies to make the dish milder and more family-friendly. (But you can add them back in if you love spicy food! Sauté them with the onions.) The cheese in this recipe is optional. See Recipe Notes below for more on that. This dish is vegetarian, no meat, but it's made with bone broth and cream, so very satisfying and good for a meatless meal.

Serves 2 to 3 (OK to double recipe).

INGREDIENTS:

2 cups young, small spinach, packed + 1 large handful

1 large onion, diced

6 ounces fontina cheese, cut into cubes 1/2-inch or smaller (see Recipe Notes)

1 cup bone broth

1/2 cup diced Roma tomatoes

1/2 cup heavy cream or fully cultured sour cream for GAPS

3 tablespoons butter

2 tablespoons grated fresh ginger

2 cloves garlic, minced or crushed

1/2 teaspoon sea salt

1/2 teaspoon garam masala

1/4 teaspoon cinnamon

1/4 teaspoon cumin

INSTRUCTIONS:

1. Melt 1 tablespoon butter in a large pan over medium-high heat. Add spinach and cook 2 minutes. Do not overcook spinach.

2. Transfer spinach to a bowl or plate to cool.

3. Add remaining 2 tablespoons butter to pan. Add onions, tomato, garlic, ginger, sea salt, cinnamon and cumin. Sauté 5 minutes, until onion is partially softened.

4. Add broth. Simmer over medium heat until mixture thickens and onions are softened, 5 more minutes.

5. While pan mixture simmers, place spinach mixture in blender. Pulse blender blade until spinach is chopped into smaller pieces. Add cream and blend again briefly to mix and purée further, about 15 seconds.

6. Transfer spinach cream mixture to simmering pan and stir to mix. Scoop half of the mixture back into the blender, reserving half in pan. Blend 20 to 25 seconds until mostly puréed. (Don't over-blend.)

7. Pour blender contents back into pan. Add remaining handful of spinach.

8. Stir and warm through over medium heat.

9. Turn off heat. Fold in cheese gently. Serve.

RECIPE NOTES:

Palaak paneer is usually made with an Indian cheese called paneer. Paneer is a fresh cheese, so it contains lactose, making it unsuitable for many wellness diets, including GAPS. Additionally, I have never found a paneer that's made from A2, pasture-raised dairy, so commercial paneers are not sustainable cheeses that are easy to digest.

I have made my recipe instead with fontina, which is a soft, aged, French cheese, made from small molecule dairy and very easy to digest for those who tolerate gentle dairy. I recommend freezing fontina for 20 to 30 minutes before using it, because it is coated in annatto, which must be cut off. The cheese is very soft, so a short freezing time makes it easier to cut off the coating and cut it into cubes.

A delicious, tangy alternative to fontina, if tolerated, is chèvre (soft goat's cheese): Crumble it on top, serve stew topped with a few slices or fold it in gently.

Cheese may also be excluded from the recipe entirely if you prefer. Three of us love the cheese in this recipe, but my youngest likes the recipe without.

Smoky Enchilada Stew

Primal, GAPS, Keto

This delicious and flavorful soup is simple and comes together surprisingly quickly, a great example of the benefit of batch cooking: If you cook the beef ahead of time or have leftover chicken, and possibly even the chile stew base, this recipe comes together in 10 minutes. If you haven't purchased dried ancho chiles before, they are sold in the ethnic foods section of almost all grocery markets. Ancho chiles are packed with nuances of flavor and are easy to work with, not very spicy and inexpensive. One bag provides several chiles, so you can store the extras in your cupboard for when you need them again.

Serves 6.

INGREDIENTS:

1-1/2 pounds ground beef, cooked up with 1-1/4 teaspoons sea salt, or 4 cups leftover chicken, chopped or shredded

7 ounces aged cheddar cheese, grated

1 cup sour cream (fully cultured for GAPS)

1/2 bunch fresh cilantro, chopped

For Stew Base:

4 cups bone broth or meat stock, hot

4 cups already cooked cauliflower (see Recipe Notes)

4 to 6 whole dried ancho chiles (depending on size), stems discarded and seeds dumped out (use gloves if desired)

1/4 cup butter or fat of choice

2 teaspoons garlic powder

1 teaspoon cumin

1-1/2 teaspoons sea salt + 1/2 teaspoon more as needed

INSTRUCTIONS:

1. In a small-medium bowl or saucepan, pour hot bone broth over the dried chiles. Cover and allow chiles to soften for 20 to 30 minutes.

2. Place chiles, bone broth, cooked cauliflower, butter, sea salt, garlic powder and cumin in blender. Purée on medium-high speed 45 to 50 seconds, until purée is smooth.

3. Combine meat and stew base in saucepan over medium heat. Stir until warmed through. Taste for salt and add up to 1/2 teaspoon more as needed.

4. Ladle into 4 dishes. Top each with equal portions sour cream, cheese and fresh cilantro.

RECIPE NOTES:

See How to Cook Cauliflower: Three Ways on Page 148. To measure: Purée, roughly mash or use 20 ounces cauliflower rice (if frozen, defrost first but no need to cook).

Easy Cold Yogurt Cucumber Soup

Primal, GAPS, GAPS Intro, Keto

This soup can also be garnished with freshly sliced or chopped radishes for added spice, nutrition and color. The walnuts are optional (but I love them!). Cold Yogurt Soup is probiotic, refreshing and satisfying.

Serves 2 to 3.

INGREDIENTS:

2 cups plain full-fat, fully cultured yogurt or probiotic sour cream

2 cups cold filtered water or no-fat (and not too solid when chilled, somewhat runny) bone broth (fat may be skimmed off the top after broth is chilled)

1 large English cucumber, peeled and finely diced

3 tablespoons fresh dill, chopped

2 tablespoons extra-virgin olive oil

1 to 2 garlic cloves, according to taste, crushed or minced

1/2 teaspoon sea salt, or more to taste

Garnish: 2 to 4 tablespoons chopped or minced walnuts (optional)

INSTRUCTIONS:

1. In a large bowl, combine cucumber, garlic, sea salt, olive oil and dill. Add yogurt, and whisk or stir to combine. Dilute gradually with cold water or broth, mixing well, making sure there are no lumps from the yogurt until the desired consistency is achieved. (You may not need all the water or broth.) Taste and add more sea salt if needed.

2. Refrigerate 30 minutes to 3 hours.

3. Serve topped with optional chopped walnuts, more diced cucumber and fresh dill.

soup-making
secrets

CHAPTER FIVE

Soup-Making Secrets

As we combine bones and meat and fat and herbs and good water,
we learn. Our knowledge of secrets increases as we make soup.
We learn to make great soup. This book shares the riches,
both read and experienced, that have evolved in my world
through years of cooking and healing. I am privileged to work
in the world of pots and bowls, to hold a wooden spoon in my hand,
to have modern implements like the Instant Pot — and to ladle.

Secret #1: Herbs

Wise ones of old gathered, dried, ground and steeped herbs — all because herbs hold powers that are mysterious only until we learn them. And then they become sacred, prized — treasures of balance and wellness.

In soups, herbs offer two benefits: flavor and nutrition. Herbs also sometimes play a third role of healing and balancing the body. Herbs are Secret #1 because they are one of my favorites.

When I rediscover a new herb by using it in a new way, I think about that herb and treasure it. I feel a sort of sober jubilation as I sip a new lemongrass broth. I ask myself: How can it be so soothing, so calming, so infused with wellness, so fully satisfying?

I feel a similar enthusiasm as I sprinkle herbs in a pot, anticipating what they will impart. While vegetables and herbs cooked for a long time in a bone broth can lead to an off-flavor, herbs added in the right way, do just the opposite.

Within the pages of this cookbook, I share with you recipes that use both dried and fresh herbs in broth, added in various ways and at different stages to optimize their best flavor and nutrition. Be sure to watch Video #2, in which I demonstrate how to properly add herbs to soups for optimal flavor.

Secret #2: Fats

The tips in this category are a true secret. I discovered the culinary techniques and benefits of using extra fat in recipes by accident, but they are used in French cooking. The French deserve their reputation for using traditional ingredients, creating amazing nuances of flavor and utilizing large amounts of fat from various parts of the animal to create rich dishes.

Outside of France, these techniques are rarely used, especially in home cooking. Americans, in particular, are often repulsed by fat. We are used to cutting it off, cutting it out or replacing it in recipes. That changed to a small extent when Dr. Natasha Campbell-McBride, who developed the GAPS diet, encouraged her patients to begin blending fatty bits and connective tissue into soups for their healing properties. Dr. Natasha helped many of us to realize that animal fats can help heal the body. What's amazing and wonderful news is that fat is also a culinary gift! Fat makes soups more satisfying, more delicious, more nuanced. Fat gives soups and stews great texture and ultimately provides that *je ne sais quoi* that no other ingredient offers.

What I discovered my second time on the GAPS Introduction diet is how many ways fat improves a soup's overall outcome. Let me explain what I then implemented into our soup café, that I believe largely contributed to our celebrated reputation in Eugene, Oregon, for having the best soup in town. When I make a soup, the fat does not come just at the beginning of a recipe, when I sauté. Fat does not come just in the middle of the soup recipe, when meat is cooked and its fat is rendered. Fat is also introduced at the very end of the soup-making process: Fat is blended in, and here the genius happens. It's all about fat.

But the yum factor also depends on what kind of fat, how it's added and at what point. The main fats that apply are olive oil, lard, schmalz, tallow, butter, ghee, bacon fat, coconut oil and sesame oil. Based on the recipe, I choose my fat. For a carrot-leek bisque, for example, I choose either bacon fat or butter. The fat gets blended into the warm meat stock and other puréed ingredients. What happens? It gently emulsifies and creates a smooth-textured, flavor-packed outcome that is not "fatty" or "greasy" — yet somehow it is MAGICAL.

With fat, we also need the right amount of sea salt, always. Taste for salt to make sure your flavors are balanced. Add more as needed. If so, you have created what most will never create: a healing, nourishing soup with a taste that I describe as incalculable. This means no one quite knows how you created a soup that tastes so good with such simple, basic ingredients — ones that most people use all the time, but perhaps not in the "right" way.

Animal fats, including butter, are the best additions to soups. Partially because they're the healthiest for most bodies, and partially because they contribute more from a culinary perspective. When to use schmalz? When to use coconut oil? Schmalz is chicken fat that's been rendered. It has all the richness of a roasted chicken and is excellent anywhere you have a rich, hearty set of ingredients: tomato-based soups, soups with winter squash, soups with beef, pork, lamb or chicken. Coconut oil, in contrast, is well suited to Asian soups and to fresh vegetable-heavy soups. Olive oil can be added to most soups, but is very rich and sometimes spicy, so should be added to taste. It is common in my book to add up to a quarter cup of fat to an almost completed soup.

Now, how to do this exactly? Watch Video #1, where I share from my kitchen how to add fats to soups to make them their best. Then experience this process yourself as you make many of the soups in this cookbook.

Secret #3: Meat Stock

When we first started the GAPS diet, about 10 years ago, I missed the concept of meat stock. I made bone broths only. Honestly, the bone broths were not super delicious. I hadn't yet learned how to prevent rancid fat from forming in long-cooked bone broth. (How to avoid rancid fat is Secret #4.) Years into the diet, I re-read *Gut and Psychology Syndrome* and learned about meat stock. Meat stock is gentler to digest. It is high in fat and rich with gelatin. Meat stock is buttery in flavor and more delicious than bone broth. Additionally, meat stock takes a lot less time to make. Therefore, I make meat stock most of time: gentler, more delicious, faster — yes, please! Using meat stock in your soups means less time and labor and a better outcome.

My favorite way to make a meat stock is in the Instant Pot. If you haven't purchased an Instant Pot or pressure cooker yet, I can't encourage you enough to acquire this helpful tool. When we moved into our tiny house, it was one of the only kitchen tools I kept. I use mine every day to make stock, soup, stew, steamed vegetables, whole chickens, pot roasts or yogurt. Stock cooks in 30 minutes in the Instant Pot (or two hours in a simmering pot) and cleans up quickly. I remember what a mess my slow-cooker used to be with bone broths constantly cooking in them.

If your budget is tight, look for a used Instant Pot. I am still using the original 6-quart machine I bought used for $35! I'd love the 8-quart and a second insert, but I keep managing fine with my first machine. I have 22 Instant Pot recipes in this book, but the pressure cooker earns its keep just by making me great, fast, tidy meat stock each week. (Most of the recipes in this cookbook do not require you to have an Instant Pot, because I didn't want to require you to have any particular tool to be able to make soup, but I do believe this cookbook is just a bit more helpful when you have one.)

Secret #4: Avoiding Rancid Fat

Most people haven't been warned about how to avoid the phenomenon that's happening in most bone broth kitchens: rancid fat. Rancid fat happens when we boil fat for a long time. How many of us throw a chicken into the slow cooker, stock pot or pressure cooker and let it cook for hours to make broth? The flavor that results is not clean. The fat has become unhealthy. Ironic, right, when we're making broth to benefit our health? Find the recipes for Bone Broth and Meat Stock in the Appendix. With each recipe, I share how to avoid rancid fat for the healthiest, best-tasting broth or stock.

Secret #5: Bisque

One more story about our early years on the GAPS diet: We ate a lot of brothy, fatty soups that weren't super yummy. Then I discovered the idea of making a bisque base for my soups, and our second time on the GAPS Intro diet was SO much easier and yummier. Of course, these same principles apply to the AIP diet, the Keto diet, all of the diets in this cookbook.

Although there are certainly times to enjoy a broth or stock-based soup, brothy soups often lose their appeal when eaten daily (or three times daily). So we make bisque! With slightly cooled broth and cooked veggies, we add a few other special ingredients, and purée. The other blended ingredients are also part of this secret: We blend in fat. (See Video #1.) We add dried or fresh herbs, and choose a theme that corresponds to the herbal flavors: Asian, Mexican or Italian, for example. (See Video #2.) We add other flavorful ingredients that don't need to be cooked, like fresh ginger. And we blend! This purée becomes the base for our soup.

Imagine how delicious a soup or stew becomes with layers of flavor added at different stages! In the puréed base, we can poach meatballs or even (gently) poach fresh fish fillets. We have an easy-to-digest, smooth, high-fat emulsion that's the opposite of boring. This bisque can deliciously be consumed on its own from a mug: Just drink it and enjoy. It can also be served in a bowl, chock-full of steamed, sautéed or roasted vegetables and various meats. Bisque-based soups don't take a long time to make, but they are often more nuanced and well-loved by eaters. More satisfying, like stew. Many of the soups in this cookbook use the blender-bisque technique. This technique is well-suited even to the GAPS Intro diet where, otherwise, meals can become mundane and leave us feeling less than satisfied emotionally.

Secret #6: Sauté

One of the reasons our café soups were so delicious is we always sautéed some of the veggies that went into the soup. Usually, we started each soup by sautéeing onions in local, grass-fed, hand-rendered tallow or extra-virgin olive oil, with sea salt. The sea salt plays a special role. By adding salt early in the sautéeing process, vegetables exude some of their water content. This step allows the vegetables to caramelize and concentrate their flavor and texture.

While starting a soup with sautéed vegetables is another important step toward creating great nuanced flavor, not all of the soups in this cookbook use the sauté step. I want some of the recipes to be just "dump and cook," easy and hands-off, in which case we gain flavor in other ways. Or we roast veggies. (Also, GAPS Intro soups do not sauté to keep the textures extra-soft.) But you'll see this step in some of the recipes and, I hope, gain an increased appreciation for its role.

Secret #7: Taste and Finish

The final secret to making great soup is learning to taste the soup at the end and then tweaking it to make it great. Every cook will execute a recipe slightly differently. So it's up to the cook at the end of the soup-making process to taste the soup before everyone else does to make sure all of the flavors are perfect.

What are you tasting for? First, taste for salt. Are the flavors coming through perfectly, or are they bland? Consider adding more sea salt, as needed. While those who will eat the soup can salt their own, it's better to serve a perfect soup. Remember to always make a properly salted meat stock or bone broth, and to salt any meat or veggies you prepare along the way, whether roasting or sautéing. While too much salt can ruin a soup, it's an art to use enough. You can cultivate this process so your end result tastes great. Adding more at the end, as needed, helps you not to over-salt along the way and to get it right in the last step.

Second, taste for fat. The soup's texture should not feel like mushy peas in your mouth. It should be velvety, pure and comforting. If the soup does not look and taste velvety, consider adding fat. You can simply stir in butter, bacon fat or your preferred fat — or you can blend some of the soup with up to a quarter cup of fat, as I demonstrate in Video #1 and discuss above in Secret #2.

Third, taste for flavor. As I touched on in Secret #1, the flavor theme should be obvious. Do you need more herbs and spices? If so, it's best not to just sprinkle them in. Rather, herbs and spices need to bloom with heat. They can be blended in if you're already blending in fat, because heat and fat help to open the herbs' flavors. Spices can be carefully toasted in a dry pan. Condiments that have been marinated in oil (like curries, tapenades or chimichurris) can be stirred into a finished soup when it's served or spooned on top. The main point is this: Consider adding more herbs and spices if the flavor profile of the soup is too mild. Are you going for Mexican? Add more cumin, onion powder, oregano and garlic. If you can have nightshades, add ancho chili powder. (Again, blend these in, don't just sprinkle them into the finished soup.) Are you going for Italian? Add more oregano, basil, garlic and olive oil. Are you creating a Greek flavor? Add fresh lemon and dried oregano, or stir in minced marinated olives and garlic. Is your dish French? If so, blend in bacon fat with thyme, sage, garlic and sea salt. What you want is to place a spoonful of the soup into your mouth and say to yourself, "Shazam! That's awesome." If you don't taste the shazam, your soup needs amending.

If the soup can't be helped with sea salt, fat, herbs or spices, you may have used a bland broth, too many mild veggies, not enough herbs or spices. Or you might have simply boiled and not sautéed your ingredients. We want concentrated and well-balanced flavors. Try to plan ahead to use concentrated, fresh broth or stock, and lots of meat or sautéed veggies — and be sure to salt along the way, not just at the end. Cultivate the ability to taste your soup and make it great every step of the way, including right before you serve. Can you save a bland soup? In addition to the tips above, keep on hand well-concentrated ingredients. For example, if you roast a chicken, save all the pan drippings and sticky bits. These can be stirred into a soup. If you tolerate miso, a spoonful or two can be stirred into an almost finished soup for a big extra scoop of umami. If the soup is Asian, not only coconut amino acids, but also fish sauce can be used. Fish sauce is a wonderful flavor enhancer in the final steps, and doesn't necessarily add a fishy flavor. Also add extra ginger and a bit of extra garlic.

To some extent you won't rely upon these secrets when using the recipes in this cookbook. The secrets are already integrated into the recipes. However, it's often helpful to know how to tweak a soup to get it just right and to know why certain steps are included and what choices make a soup better or great. These tips also help you to make your own soups with ingredients you have on hand.

Bonus Secret: Love

It may be corny hippie wisdom, but I always prefer eating a soup made by a passionate heart and hand. Bring love and passion to your kitchen. Infuse your soups with YOU and with a desire to nourish those you're feeding. Love is as important as skill, experience and sea salt.

Visit my blog, E A T   B E A U T I F U L (www.eatbeautiful.net/secrets-free-videos) to access Video #1 and #2.

Broths and Stocks

When I make bone broth, I always make meat stock first. The initial cooking time of bone broth renders a significant amount of fat that should not cook for an extended period of time. The fat from the initial cooking time needs to be skimmed off and saved or included in the harvested meat stock. If the fat continues to boil, it will become rancid. For stovetop or slow cooker bone broth, this time period is 2 to 3 hours. For Instant Pot or pressure cooker broth, this time period is 30 minutes.

Meat stock is the first batch of broth that comes off of fatty or meaty bones. We collect this stock, which is very high in gelatin and oftentimes fat and has a rich flavor. Then we add more water and sea salt and continue cooking the bones to yield a longer-cooked bone broth. Meat stock can also be made from bones with all their meat still intact, such as chicken drumsticks, a whole chicken or meaty ribs. This method allows you to harvest and use the meat as well as the broth, so it's a nice time saver. This method yields an especially delicious stock.

Some people choose to combine their stock and broth batches. Broth contains more protein than stock. Meat stock is best for those with more fragile digestion. The GAPS Introduction diet utilizes meat stock. I prefer the flavor, gentleness and role of meat stock and frequently make just stock for our family. While bone broth is more famous, I use meat stock more often. It's a daily staple in our home for drinking from a mug or using in soups. I enjoy the buttery, rich flavor of meat stock and as mentioned, how well it digests. Meat stock is also faster and easier to make. Bone broth is ideal for soups that need a long cook time or for those desiring the extra protein. This cookbook calls for the use of both stock and broth, depending on its role in a recipe and your preference.

Stovetop, Slow Cooker and Instant Pot/Pressure Cooker Instructions

INGREDIENTS:

For Stovetop or Slow Cooker:

3 pounds bones and cartilage from: organic or pasture-raised chicken, grass-finished beef bones or other sustainable animal bones, joints preferred, or exposed marrow

2 tablespoons raw apple cider vinegar, optional (not ideal for those with FODMAP or fructose sensitivities)

1 to 1-1/2 gallons filtered water (this amount of water allows for some evaporation during the cooking time; more water may be added as needed)

2 tablespoons sea salt (adjust according to pot size and to taste)

For Instant Pot/Pressure Cooker:

10 cups filtered water (you will need 20 cups water total if you choose Option 2 below)

3 pounds bones and cartilage from: organic or pasture-raised chicken, grass-finished beef bones or other sustainable animal bones, joints preferred, or exposed marrow

2 tablespoons sea salt

INSTRUCTIONS:

For Stovetop or Slow Cooker:

1. Add bones to pot or slow cooker.

2. Fill with filtered water. Add optional apple cider vinegar and sea salt.

3. Cook 2-1/2 to 3 hours (adjust heat so stock simmers).

4. Harvest all the fat, or fatty broth. This is meat stock.

RECIPE NOTES:

If you harvest all of the broth (not just the fat from the surface), add new water, salt, and apple cider vinegar and simmer on low at least 24 hours and up to 72 hours to make broth. (Within 30 minutes of the broth's first boiling, scum may rise to the surface; skim this off.) Strain and use.

INSTANT POT INSTRUCTIONS:

1. Place water in pot. (Optional: Add Steamer Basket to more easily strain stock when it's finished cooking.) Add bones and sea salt. Seal lid and close steam valve. Press "Soup" button.

2. When timer goes off, allow 60 minutes for the pressure to release naturally.

3. Press "Cancel" button and carefully open steam valve. Open lid.

4. **Option 1:** Use a ladle or spoon to scoop the fat off the top of the stock. Save fat for another use. **Option 2:** When meat stock and pot are cool enough to handle, pour the entire contents of pot (fat and stock) through a fine mesh sieve into storage jars, reserving the bones to make bone broth.

VARIATIONS:

For Low-Histamine Stock: Use stock from the first 2 to 3 hours of cooking on the stovetop or in a slow cooker. Use stock from the first 30 minutes of cooking in an Instant Pot. The bones must be very fresh, or frozen very fresh.

For Bone Marrow Meat Stock: Follow instructions for Meat Stock, but use 3 pounds marrow bones. When stock is finished cooking, use a handheld colander spoon to remove bones, marrow and meat solids from stock. Or pour stock through a fine mesh sieve into storage containers. If using an Instant Pot or pressure cooker, use Steamer Basket for easy harvesting of bones. Set bones and marrow aside to cool. Store stock in refrigerator. When cool enough to handle, jolt the marrow from each bone by thumping it hard on the counter. (Some of the marrow may fall out into the stock on its own.) In most cases, the marrow will easily fall out. Use cracked crab tools or a small spoon or knife to scoop out any marrow that doesn't come out easily. The bones may be used again to make bone broth with fresh water and sea salt.

RECIPE NOTES:

You now have either a pot with stock (almost no fat) and bones (**Option 1**), or you have an empty pot (**Option 2**). **Option 1** will give you less overall stock and broth in the end, but a lot of nutrients will be concentrated into one rich

meat stock. **Option 2** will give you two batches: one, a meat stock that's high in fat and gelatin, rich and flavorful. And two, a bone broth without much fat but high in protein. Both variations are great and fine and just a matter of preference. Most importantly, we aren't allowing the fat to have a long cooking time, during which time it becomes rancid and bad-tasting. With **Option 1**, the fat is now removed. We'll simply continue cooking the broth now (next recipe), to extract extra protein from the bones with the longer cooking time.

Bone Broth

Stovetop, Slow Cooker and Instant Pot/Pressure Cooker Instructions

INGREDIENTS:

For Stovetop or Slow Cooker:

broth and bones remaining after fat is removed from meat stock

water, as needed

sea salt, adjusted for taste and pot size

2 tablespoons raw apple cider vinegar, optional (not ideal for those with FODMAP or fructose sensitivities)

INSTRUCTIONS:

For Stovetop or Slow Cooker:

1. Cook broth an additional 24 to 72 hours.

2. Skim off any scum that rises to the surface within 30 minutes of the broth's first boiling.

3. Strain and store in refrigerator until ready to use.

INSTANT POT INSTRUCTIONS:

1. **Option 1:** After fat is removed from stock, reseal lid.

2. **Option 2:** Return strained bones to the pot. Add 2 tablespoons additional sea salt and 10 cups additional filtered water.

3. Turn steam valve to closed position. Choose "Manual" button, then "-" button to set time at 120 minutes.

4. When timer goes off, allow pressure to release naturally for 1 hour minimum.

5. Open steam valve carefully to release any remaining steam.

6. Strain and store in refrigerator until ready to use.

Shrimp Shell Stock

The easiest way to get shrimp shells for stock is to ask your fishmonger for the shells. Some fish markets remove and discard the shells. Our local fish shop charges a tiny price for shrimp shells. Alternately, whole shrimp can be blanched. I give instructions for using whole shrimp in the Variation below. Shrimp stock is best consumed within two days of being made.

INGREDIENTS:

2 pounds shrimp shells, or 2 pounds large raw shrimp

1 tablespoon bacon fat, lard, butter or extra-virgin olive oil

8 cups water

2 teaspoons sea salt

INSTRUCTIONS:

1. In a stock pot, heat fat. Add shells and cook over medium-high heat until they turn pink, about 8 minutes.

2. Add water and salt and turn heat to high. Bring water to a boil, then reduce heat so broth simmers slowly. Simmer 30 minutes.

3. Strain into heat-proof bowl through fine mesh sieve, pressing on solids to extract as much liquid as possible. Use immediately or chill.

VARIATION:

To make stock with whole shrimp, heat 8 cups water in large stock pot over high heat. Bring water to a boil. Add shrimp. When water returns to a boil, simmer 5 to 7 minutes. Using slotted spoon, remove shrimp to ice water. Peel shrimp, returning shells to stock pot. (Set shrimp aside for another use.) Bring stock pot water (with shrimp shells) back to a boil. Simmer 30 minutes, then follow Step 3 above.

Fish Stock

Fish stock is made like meat stock — with a short cook time. Thirty minutes of stovetop simmering is all that is needed, and fish stocks are best enjoyed the day they're made. (Shrimp stock is also good the next day.) Regarding salt, we start with half the amount we would use for a meat stock, and add more to taste, if needed, when the stock is done cooking.

INGREDIENTS:

8 to 10 cups water

2 to 3 pounds fish bones

1 tablespoon sea salt

INSTRUCTIONS:

1. To a large stock pot, add water, fish bones and salt.

2. Turn heat to high. Bring water to a boil, then cover and reduce heat so broth simmers slowly. Simmer 30 minutes.

3. Strain into heat-proof bowl through fine mesh sieve, pressing on solids to extract as much liquid as possible.

4. Add freshly grated ginger, crushed garlic and/ or steep fresh herbs in the finished stock.

Bonito Stock

Not GAPS Intro

Bonito can be purchased at Asian or natural grocery markets. There are only two ingredients in traditional bonito broth, called dashi, other than water: kombu and bonito. For our purposes, as a substitution for long-cooking bone broth, bonito broth can be made without the kombu, for a less oceanic flavor. (Traditionally, in Japan, it is just the opposite: Dashi can be made with kombu alone; or the nourishing bonito can be added optionally to make a more complete broth.) Each portion of bonito flakes used to make broth can be used twice, once for a mild broth, and a second time for a richer, darker broth. Very economical. The recipe I provide includes kombu as an optional ingredient, if you want the Asian flavor and added nutrition. In traditional Japanese cooking, these almost sacred broths, which serve as the foundation for almost all their dishes, are called First Dashi and Second Dashi.

Bonito flakes are shavings of dried, fermented, smoked tuna. Because the shavings come from the whole fish, bones are included. It is not fishy tasting. The flavor is smoky and mild. Dashi traditionally makes a great base for miso soup; but I've even made beef stew with it and you don't know it's there. Is it safe to consume fish, especially tuna, based on concerns with mercury and the 2011 radiation leak off the coast of Japan? Bonito flakes come from skipjack tuna that do not swim or migrate anywhere near the coastal waters of Japan. Tuna in general has been vindicated in regard to its levels of mercury. Health advocates and functional practitioners tell us mercury is not problematic if it is in the right ratio to selenium in the fish itself, which is the case with tuna.

Yields 8 cups.

INGREDIENTS:

2 quarts filtered water plus 2 quarts more water for second batch
1 cup packed bonito flakes
1 ounce dried kombu, optional

INSTRUCTIONS:

1. Place optional kombu in saucepan with water. Heat but do not let water boil.

2. As bubbles appear in hot water, just before it simmers, remove optional kombu, setting it aside.

3. Add bonito flakes. Keep heat on under pot and allow water to come to a boil. Then turn heat off immediately. Bonito flakes will absorb water and slowly sink. Allow 3 to 5 minutes for this process.

4. Strain broth, reserving bonito. This is First Dashi.

5. For a second, stronger broth, put 2 quarts more water back into pot with reserved kombu and bonito. Heat water to barely a simmer (do not boil) for 10 minutes.

6. Strain. This is Second Dashi.

RECIPE NOTES:

If you are on the GAPS Introduction diet, kombu is not allowed.

Fresh Herb Broth

While a French press isn't necessary, making fresh herb broth in a French press is effective and elevates the ritual. Whatever your vessel, fresh herb broth is delicious and special, as well as healthful.

Serves 2 to 4.

INGREDIENTS:

4 cups bone broth or meat stock

1/4 to 1/2 cup fresh herbs of choice: rosemary, thyme, mint, grated ginger or other favorite

INSTRUCTIONS:

1. In medium-size saucepan, heat broth or stock until it just begins to simmer.

2. While heating, add fresh herb of choice to bottom of French press (see Recipe Notes).

3. Pour hot broth into French press. Place the top on the beaker with the plunger pulled all the way up to help keep the temperature up while the herbs steep. Allow herbs to steep 10 minutes.

4. Gently press the plunger all the way down.

5. Pour broth into mugs and enjoy.

RECIPE NOTES:

If you don't have a French press, simply steep herbs in the saucepan or individual mugs.

Chinese Wellness Broth

(an Instant Pot recipe)

This traditional broth is actually a stock, good for invalids — nourishing and flavorful. I make mine in the Instant Pot because it's a hands-off process, which means less stress and more wellness for the cook! :)

The ingredients in Chinese broths vary depending on one's health and if a patient has seen a Chinese herbalist. I like to include ginger, for digestive support and its warming and anti-inflammatory benefits. I include codonopsis root, which is calming, aids digestion, improves circulation, supports the HPA axis (supports adrenals and combats mental and physical tiredness) and helps to relieve stress. Shitake mushrooms are another great option. Shiitakes help to regulate the immune system, detoxify and restore. Lastly, I include garlic for its anti-inflammatory, anti-microbial and antioxidant benefits. Although codonopsis root is harder to source than the other ingredients, I encourage you to include it. The benefits of this adaptogenic herb go beyond what I've mentioned here and are just so good for those of us who need to reduce stress, boost energy and improve mental health. (A few of the additional potential benefits include improvements for lung health, urinary health, blood sugar levels, inflammation and aging.)

The flavor of this stock is slightly spicy from the ginger and absolutely yummy. I find it restorative while being calming.

INGREDIENTS:

10 cups water

3 pounds chicken meat and bones

1 cup fresh shiitake mushrooms or 12 to 15 dried shiitake mushrooms

3 tablespoons fresh ginger root, roughly chopped

4 cloves garlic

2 tablespoons sea salt

.15 ounces codonopsis root (see Recipe Notes)

INSTRUCTIONS:

1. Place all ingredients into Instant Pot. (Optional: Insert steamer basket into Instant Pot first. See Recipe Notes.) Seal lid and shut steam valve. Press "Soup" button.

2. When timer goes off, allow pressure to release naturally 60 minutes minimum. Press "Cancel" and carefully open steam valve.

3. Open lid. Remove solids using steamer basket or handheld colander spoon.

4. If you wish, chop up codonopsis root (edible and soft like carrots when cooked) and slice shiitake mushrooms.

5. Remove chicken from the bones.

6. Make a nice soup with these ingredients and the broth, or simply enjoy the broth on its own.

RECIPE NOTES:

The chicken skin and cartilage may also be saved and used in soup recipes (see the blender bisque method discussed in the Secrets chapter).

See Resource Guide for my steamer basket recommendations, Page 161.

See Resource Guide for links to source codonopsis root, Page 162.

BASIC COOKED VEGETABLES FOR USE IN SOUPS

How and Why to Bake Onions

Roasting whole or halved onions is a handy approach to making dinner both flavorful and fast. Peeling and chopping onions to then sauté can be a time-consuming series of steps, not to mention the tears! Roasting halved onions cuts your time down considerably and yields a wonderful texture and complexity to a soup's base. I use this method often, and it can even be used on the GAPS Introduction diet because the onion's skin keeps the inside onion soft.

INSTRUCTIONS:

1. Preheat oven to 375 degrees Fahrenheit.

2. Grease a large cookie sheet by rubbing with preferred fat (ghee, animal fat or avocado oil).

3. Cut desired number of onions in half, removing any outer skin that is particularly loose. (Keep on any skin that adheres well, as it will be easier to remove once baked, and it will protect the soft onion inside from getting tough.)

4. Place halved onions skin side up (cut side down) on prepared cookie sheet.

5. Bake onions 45 minutes until outside skin is darkened and flaky, and inside is completely tender.

6. Remove from oven and allow to cool slightly before peeling off outer layers of skin. The onions are now ready for use in any soup recipe.

RECIPE NOTES:

Baked onions are great puréed into soup bases. You can even batch cook these onions once a week and have them on hand for soups.

How to prevent crying when cutting onions: If your onions are particularly vaporous and causing you to cry, you can actually freeze them for 15 minutes. This step freezes the vapors that cause us to tear up! I halve mine first, then lay them on a cookie sheet cut side up. Place them in the freezer for 15 minutes, then proceed with peeling and chopping them.

How to Roast Whole Carrots

Roasted carrots are a valuable but thrifty ingredient. At our café, we often baked up several trays of juicing carrots for a big batch of soup. Roasted carrots can be puréed into a bisque base or diced up and added for rich texture. Roasting carrots saves time and enhances the soup's flavor.

INGREDIENTS:

2 pounds whole carrots
1/4 cup extra-virgin olive oil or fat of choice
1-1/2 teaspoons sea salt

INSTRUCTIONS:

1. Preheat oven to 350 degrees Fahrenheit.
2. Toss carrots in fat and sea salt and place on a baking sheet lined with parchment paper.
3. Roast 50 to 60 minutes (depending on carrots' size), or until tender when pierced with a knife.

VARIATION:

You may also roast carrots at 400 or 425 degrees Fahrenheit, but I find they're sweeter when cooked longer at the lower temperature.

How to Cook Cauliflower: Three Ways

This section shares how to cook cauliflower so that it is already prepared for use in recipes. Cauliflower is frequently used in wellness diet recipes. Puréed, it can help to create a creamy base. Roasted and added to soups, it contributes a nice flavor and texture. Cauliflower rice is a great soup thickener or side dish.

STEAMING INSTRUCTIONS:

1. Cut off outer leaves of cauliflower. Remove the core from the cauliflower and roughly chop it into individual florets.
2. Bring about 2 inches of water to a boil in the bottom of a pot into which your steamer basket or insert fits.
3. Add chopped cauliflower to steam insert. Cover pot.
4. Steam cauliflower until fork tender, about 10 minutes.

INSTANT POT INSTRUCTIONS:

1. Add steamer basket to the bottom of Instant Pot (see Recipe Notes). Add 1 cup of water.
2. Cut off outer leaves of cauliflower. Remove the core from the cauliflower and roughly chop it into individual florets.
3. Add chopped cauliflower to steamer basket. Close the lid and seal the steam valve. Use the "Manual" button to cook on high pressure for 3 minutes.
4. After the cooking cycle is finished, do a quick pressure release: Turn the venting knob from the sealed position to the venting position. When all the pressure is released, open the lid.

ROASTING INSTRUCTIONS:

1. Preheat the oven to 450 degrees Fahrenheit.
2. Cut 2 heads cauliflower into bite-size florets (about 8 cups).
3. Toss cauliflower with 1/4 cup extra-virgin olive oil or preferred fat and 1-1/2 teaspoons sea salt. Spread onto baking sheet lined with parchment paper.
4. Roast until golden and tender, about 20 minutes.

RECIPE NOTES:

See Resource Guide for steamer basket recommendations, Page 161.

How to Bake Winter Squash

INGREDIENTS:

1 butternut squash (weighing 2 to 4 pounds)

INSTRUCTIONS:

1. Preheat oven to 375 degrees Fahrenheit.

2. Place winter squash on large baking sheet to catch any drippings.

3. Bake 1 hour or until very tender when poked through the neck with a long knife.

4. Cut squash in half. Remove seeds from cavity. Use a vegetable peeler or paring knife to remove outer skin.

5. Place soft lower portion of flesh from around the seed cavity in blender (with designated broth and other ingredients) to create a bisque base. Cube the remaining neck flesh for the body of the soup.

BASIC MEATBALLS
FOR USE IN SOUPS

Ground Meat and Herb Meatballs

Meatballs turn sometimes-mundane ground meat into many people's favorite comfort food. By varying herbs and spices, meatballs can compliment a variety of ethnic dishes, from Latin to Italian to Asian. Meatballs are economical and also easy to digest for most. For those on GAPS Intro, follow the Poaching Instructions below. Otherwise, choose the cooking instructions below that match your recipe or lifestyle: Simmer the meatballs in your broth or bisque base, or bake them in the oven and add them to your main dish soup or stew.

Recipe can be doubled or tripled by ratio.

INGREDIENTS:

1 pound ground meat of choice

1 teaspoon sea salt

1-1/2 teaspoons dried herbs

POACHING INSTRUCTIONS:

1. In a large bowl (or atop butcher paper packaging that meat came in), stir together meat, salt and herbs for 2 to 3 minutes, until herbs look fairly evenly distributed.

2. Form meatballs into desired shaped balls, 1 to 1-1/2 inches in circumference. Place onto a large plate.

3. Bring broth or bisque to a slow simmer over medium heat. A large deep skillet may be used or a medium-large saucepan.

4. Add meatballs, without over-crowding. Simmer gently, occasionally stirring to move meatballs around. See Poaching Guide for length of cooking time, Page 153.

BAKING INSTRUCTIONS:

1. Preheat oven to 375 degrees Fahrenheit.

2. In a large bowl (or atop butcher paper packaging that meat came in), stir together meat, salt and herbs for 2 to 3 minutes, until herbs look fairly evenly distributed.

3. Form meatballs into desired shaped balls, 1 to 1-1/2 inches in circumference. Place into greased oven-safe skillet.

4. Bake 10 to 15 minutes, depending on meat variety: For poultry (such as chicken and turkey), bake 15 minutes. For well-done red meat, bake 15 minutes. For more nutritious red meat, cook to medium doneness, 10 minutes for beef, lamb, buffalo and wild game.

Seafood or Shellfish Meatballs

INGREDIENTS:

1 pound fish or shellfish (salmon, cod, sole, shrimp, scallops, etc.), fresh or frozen and defrosted

2 tablespoons cassava flour or tapioca flour (for GAPS and Keto, use 1 egg yolk instead; see VAD variation below)

1 tablespoon fresh herb of choice (parsley, cilantro, tarragon, etc.), chopped into smaller pieces

1 teaspoon sea salt

1 teaspoon garlic powder

1 teaspoon dried herb of choice (basil, oregano, dill, etc.)

1/2 teaspoon spice of choice (ginger, cumin)

INSTRUCTIONS:

1. If using fish fillets, cut them into smaller pieces, no larger than 1 inch by 2 inches.

2. Place seafood in blender or food processor. Top seafood with fresh herb.

3. In small bowl, stir together flour (or egg yolks), sea salt, garlic, dried herb and spice. Pour flour mixture on top of seafood and herb in blender. Pulse until seafood is chopped into small pieces (like ground meat) and flour mixture is evenly incorporated.

4. When ready to cook meatballs, bring broth or bisque to a slow simmer.

5. Use a small cookie dough scoop or two spoons to form balls. Make each ball about 1 inch in circumference.

6. Add seafood meatballs to simmering broth. Cook 10 to 12 minutes. Remove one to a plate and cut it open if you're not sure if they're done. Seafood meatballs will be light and aerated when fully cooked, and the fish, in most cases, will look more yellow-white instead of grey-white.

VARIATION:

For VAD: Use only sole, flounder or seafood you feel confident is free of vitamin A and from clean waters. No deep, cold-water fish. Use salt, pepper and garlic to season. You may also add ginger and turmeric. Use the tapioca flour option.

OTHER BASICS FOR USE IN SOUPS

How to Poach Meat + Boil Eggs

One of the easiest ways to cook meat when you're preparing gentle, nourishing soups is to poach it. While boiling meat has an expectedly bad connotation, poaching is the gourmet cousin of this approach. Simply place your meat of choice into slowly simmering bone broth and allow it to cook. Cooking times and testing for doneness is based on the kind of meat. The following chart will help you, but the cut size of meat will make cooking times vary. To be sure, always remove one piece of meat and either cut it open in the center; or with chicken, poke it through to the center. You want chicken juices to run clear, no pink blood. Other kinds of meat are more nutritious and taste better if they're undercooked on purpose, like beef, lamb and salmon. Don't overcook these gems. Learn to like medium-rare meat.

1-1/2-inch diameter meatballs of lamb, beef or bison	15 minutes
1-1/2-inch diameter meatballs of turkey or other poultry	20 minutes
1/4-pound fillets of salmon	5 to 8 minutes
large shrimp or prawns	5 to 8 minutes
2-1/2-inch diameter backstrap of red meat animal, such as elk, deer, beef, lamb or bison	15 to 20 minutes
2-1/2-inch diameter pork tenderloin	20 to 25 minutes
beef steak or fillet	10 minutes
chicken drumsticks or thighs	30 to 35 minutes
chicken breasts	25 to 30 minutes (Or cut thickness in half and poach 10 minutes.)
whole chicken or rabbit	1 to 1-1/4 hours (Test for doneness by poking the thigh deeply to the bone; look for clear juices.)
hard-boiled eggs	12 minutes (Bring water to a boil first; then simmer 12 to 14 minutes.)
soft-boiled eggs	6 minutes (Bring water to a boil first; then simmer 6 to 8 minutes, depending on how runny you want your yolk.)

How to Poach or Fry Eggs

Fried eggs are nice because they're casual, fast and impromptu. Poached eggs are more elegant and impressive (if that's important for your meal, which for most of us it isn't), and perhaps more importantly: They can 1) be prepared ahead of time if you enjoy batch cooking, and simply heated in a moment by placing them in very hot water or 2) be kept hot in warm water until you're ready to serve, which isn't possible with fried eggs. Lastly, the texture plays a part. Sometimes I poach my eggs just because I love that silky smooth texture. But I like and choose both options, depending on the situation. Of course, fried eggs are a bit easier, and that often wins out!

POACHING INSTRUCTIONS:

1. Crack each egg separately into a (small) bowl or saucer.

2. Bring a pan of water filled at least 2 inches deep to a simmer. Add a drop of vinegar.

3. Reduce the heat beneath the pan, and slide in 1 egg at a time: Slowly tip the first egg into the center of the pan. Maintain the right heat under your pan so there are small bubbles rising.

4. Once the egg begins to set, gently push it to one side of the pan.

5. Add your next eggs in the same manner as the first.

6. As each one cooks (about 3 to 4 minutes), lift the egg out with a slotted spoon and drain it on a dish towel.

7. If you wish, trim off any straggly bits from the edges, and keep it at the right temperature in warm water.

FRYING INSTRUCTIONS:

1. Heat pan over medium-high heat. Add 1 tablespoon avocado oil.

2. Crack each egg into the pan.

3. Add 1/4 cup water to pan (optional).

4. Season eggs lightly with sea salt. Cover the pan with a lid, and cook 3 minutes over low heat.

5. Check that the white is set and, if not, cook for another 30 seconds; then check again.

How to Soak Seeds or Nuts

INSTRUCTIONS:

1. For every 4 cups of raw seeds or nuts, cover with room temperature, filtered water by 2 inches and 2 teaspoons sea salt. Stir well to dissolve the salt.

2. Leave out overnight at room temperature to soak.

3. Drain seeds or nuts in a colander and rinse them well.

RECIPE NOTES:

If you suspect old nuts, possible rancidity or mold, such as with peanuts, add 1/2 teaspoon vitamin C powder to the salted soaking water. This will kill any potential mold.

Cashews and seeds need a shorter soaking time of 2 to 6 hours.

How to Use Fresh Lemongrass

INSTRUCTIONS:

1. To use whole lemongrass stalk, cut off the top of the stalk. Make a few vertical slices in it; then set it aside.

2. Peel off the outer layers of the bottom 3 inches. Here you'll find a paler, more tender core.

3. Cut off the end (the lower bulb) and discard.

4. Using a rolling pin or the butt of knife or similar kitchen tool, smash to soften the root and release flavors. Smash top of stalk, as well.

5. Add this smashed base as well as the top of the stalk to water or broth before cooking to release flavors.

6. Lemongrass is fibrous, so guests can remove stalk as they eat. Alternatively, the softer, pale bottom of the stalk (the 2 to 3 inches that are softest) may be minced and eaten after cooking, if preferred.

RECIPE NOTES:

Select fresh lemongrass stalks that are heavy, tightly formed, fragrant and firm with little or no bruising. The lower half of the stalk should be lemony-green.

Tip: Lemongrass freezes well, so you may find whole stalks in the freezer section of Asian grocery stores.

Instant Pot Tips

QUICK RELEASE TIPS:

Doing a Quick Pressure Release (QPR or QR) can speed up the soup-making process, which for many of us is a big part of the Instant Pot's convenience. To make this option safer (and quieter), try opening the steam valve only halfway. The steam will take longer to escape, but the process is less "exuberant." You can then proceed to the next step in your soup-making process more quickly.

Avoid doing a quick release when the pot is completely full. Give the steam 30 to 60 minutes or longer to release naturally, avoiding unnecessary sputtering from the steam valve (the contents of the pot are still boiling inside).

I also recommend the Steam Boss tool, sold as an accessory to the Instant Pot. The Steam Boss directs steam away from kitchen cabinets and makes the quick release process safer and less messy. (See product link in Resource Guide.)

STEAMING TIPS:

Place steamer basket and 2 cups of water into Instant Pot. Press "Sauté" button. The water will reach a simmer in 5 to 6 minutes. Place the glass lid onto the Instant Pot to allow the water to reach a boil faster.

Add vegetables to the steamer basket and re-cover the pot with lid. Steam to desired doneness.

Glass Canning Jar Tips

I don't know if you've experienced this, but I have: Glass canning jars can break when hot broth is poured into them — or in the freezer when the contents expand. Here are tips to help you avoid both of these inconveniences.

POURING HOT BROTH INTO GLASS JARS:

Place a metal implement (a spoon, knife or fork) into the jar. Pour the hot broth in. The metal will absorb some of the heat and help prevent the jar from breaking.

FREEZING BROTH IN GLASS JARS:

Fill the jar with broth or soup, but leave 3 inches headroom at the top. Screw on lid. Place the jar in the freezer on its side. This creates a greater surface area, so when the soup expands the jar won't break.

Nomato Sauce

Stovetop and Instant Pot Instructions

INGREDIENTS:

For Stovetop:

4 medium carrots, cut in half

1 small beet

1 small turnip

2/3 cup bone broth or meat stock

3 tablespoons lime or lemon juice (or 1 drop lemongrass essential oil if citrus isn't tolerated)

1-inch piece fresh ginger, roughly chopped

1-1/2-inch piece fresh turmeric, roughly chopped (or use 1/2 teaspoon turmeric powder)

2 cloves fresh garlic, roughly chopped

1 teaspoon dried oregano

1/4 teaspoon sea salt

For Instant Pot (makes a larger batch):

8 medium-size carrots, unpeeled

2 small- to medium-size beets, unpeeled

2 small- to medium-size onions, unpeeled

1-1/3 cups bone broth

1/4 cup + 2 tablespoons lime or lemon juice (or 1 to 2 drops lemongrass essential oil if citrus isn't tolerated)

2 tablespoons fresh ginger root, grated and then measured

4 cloves garlic, smashed or minced

1 tablespoon dried oregano

1 teaspoon dried basil

1/2 teaspoon sea salt

INSTRUCTIONS:

1. Cook veggies until they're very tender: carrots, turnip and beets. (Steam, roast or cook them in simmering water or broth.)

2. Place the 2/3 cup bone broth in blender. Add slightly cooled, cooked veggies. Add remaining ingredients as well: lime juice, ginger, turmeric, garlic, oregano and sea salt.

3. Purée until smooth, 30 to 50 seconds. You will have a thick, beautiful sauce to use in soups and stews.

INSTANT POT INSTRUCTIONS:

1. Place carrots, beets and onions into Instant Pot insert. Add bone broth. Close lid and seal steam valve. Press the "Manual" setting, and decrease the time using the "-" button until you reach 15 minutes.

2. When the Instant Pot is done and beeps, press "Cancel." Allow Instant Pot to release pressure naturally, about 30 minutes.

3. Carefully open steam valve. Remove lid and insert, so the pot's contents begin to cool.

4. Using a slotted spoon, remove veggies to large plate to cool slightly. When cool enough to handle, slide skins off onions, composting or discarding the peel.

5. Cut beets and onions in half, or allow onions to fall apart in layers. Place all veggies in blender. Add warm broth, garlic, ginger, lime juice (or lemongrass), dried herbs and sea salt. Purée 30 seconds on medium-high speed. Stop partway through and scrape down the sides of blender jar, if needed. Resume puréeing until smooth. The sauce is now ready to be used in any recipe.

RESOURCE GUIDE

Recommended Cooking Tools

What supplies are needed to make soup? On a tight budget, not much! History tells us soup can be made with just a pot and a spoon. But if you'd like to furnish your kitchen with some soup-making resources, I share here the supplies I use often and consider to be the most important.

You'll see these supplies called for throughout the pages of the cookbook: (a) stock pot, (b) large and small saucepans, (c) handheld colander spoon, (d) Instant Pot, (e) Instant Pot Steamer Basket, (f) Instant Pot Steam Boss, (g) fine mesh strainers, (h) metal spatula, (i) ladle, (j) serving spoon, (k) French press, (l) wooden spoon/spatula, (m) blender [ideally not made of plastic], (n) spiralizer, (o) slotted spoon

Visit my blog, E A T   B E A U T I F U L (www.eatbeautiful.net/soup-tools-ingredients), where I provide links to recommended products.

Recommended Ingredients

Occasionally, specific ingredients can be hard to find. I've listed those ingredients here, and you can find links to the products on my website.

• Organic ancho chili powder or dried whole ancho chiles
• Cajun seasoning
• Codonopsis root
• Collagen
• Cordyceps mushroom powder
• Basil and lemongrass essential oil
• Organic Harvest Foods' red Jalapeño Pepper Sauce
• Paleo protein powders
• Palm oil shortening (by Grain Brain)
• Perfect Supplements Bone Broth powder (in a pinch or when you're traveling)
• Real fermented soy sauce
• Shiro Miso fermented miso paste
• Sour cream: For GAPS, use fully cultured sour cream or lactose-free sour cream in place of heavy cream. Nancy's brand is fully cultured; Green Valley Organics is lactose-free.
• Sprouted lentils

Visit my blog, E A T B E A U T I F U L (www.eatbeautiful.net/soup-tools-ingredients), where I provide links to recommended products.

Glossary of Diets

The following information is a quick synopsis about each of the diets featured in this cookbook. The discussion also touches on low-FODMAP, low-histamine and lectin-free dietary requirements, so that those of you who are following any of these restricted diets can apply the concepts to the recipes in this cookbook simply by substituting one ingredient for another.

PALEO/PRIMAL

This ancestral diet is grain-free and refined sugar-free. *Paleo* means no processed foods and eating with the seasons. If a recipe is Paleo and contains dairy (other than butter or as a garnish), it is designated as *Primal*.

GAPS DIET

GAPS stands for "Gut and Psychology Syndrome," a diet created by Dr. Natasha Campbell-McBride. The GAPS diet is grain-free and refined sugar-free, and it focuses on high-fat, soft-textured soups and stews. Starchy foods are removed from GAPS recipes — which means, for example, no sweet potatoes or parsnips. The GAPS diet is intended to address and improve mental health issues, as well as to provide gut-healing benefits. If you see a recipe designated as *GAPS+*, this means to look for a small number of modifications within the recipe to make it compliant. For example, you might see a note to omit an ingredient like tapioca flour, or to substitute sweet potato with winter squash.

GAPS INTRO

The GAPS Introduction diet is a more restricted version of the GAPS diet. GAPS Intro is an elimination diet that emphasizes gentle meat stocks over bone broths, and simmered soups instead of baked, sautéed or grilled foods. The elimination stages of this diet remove eggs, dairy and many other foods. The eliminated foods get added back in or challenged gradually. Key aspects of *GAPS Intro* soup recipes include: They are always cooked gently, they exclude certain vegetables and textures that may be abrasive, and they are usually high in fat.

AIP

AIP refers to Autoimmune Protocol. This diet is designed to reduce inflammation and help put autoimmune diseases into remission. The AIP diet is an offshoot of the Paleo diet. In addition to grain-free and refined sugar-free guidelines, AIP is egg-free, nut-free, dairy-free and nightshade-free, with several other specifications, as well. The *AIP* recipes in this cookbook will always be free of the above potentially inflammatory foods. If you see a recipe designated *AIP+*, this means to look for a small number of modifications within the recipe to make it compliant. For example, you might see a note to omit an ingredient like pepper, or substitute maple syrup for stevia.

KETO

The Keto diet denotes ketogenic recipes high in fat and low in carbohydrates. Protein quantities vary and can be determined by individual cooks based on personal dietary goals. The Keto diet can help with weight loss, health goals and significant health challenges including epilepsy and cancer. This recipe collection includes both dairy and dairy-free *Keto* soups and stews. If a recipe is designated *Keto+*, look for a small number of modifications to make the recipe low-carb. For example, you might see a note to omit carrots from a recipe or to sub in fennel in place of onion.

VAD

The Vitamin A Detox diet is the newest remedial diet to impact patients with leaky gut, autoimmune diseases and symptoms that are hard to resolve such as eczema, mental health and vision problems. This diet removes all foods high or moderate in vitamin A, allowing the liver to detoxify excess vitamin A and resolve symptoms over time. This is the diet I'm currently using to address my health challenges. Read more about the *VAD* diet and get a printable grocery list from my blog. Type "VAD" or "VAD grocery list" into the search engine at EatBeautiful.net. If a recipe is designated *VAD+*, look for a small number of modifications to make the recipe low in vitamin A or to remove resistant starch. For example, you may be guided to use tapioca flour instead of cassava flour, or you may see a note to omit or exchange one vegetable for another.

LOW-FODMAP

FODMAP is an acronym referring to four types of foods that, if not well digested in the small intestine, can ferment in the large intestine. (These foods are classified as Fermentable Oligo-, Di-, Mono-saccharides And Polyols. By temporarily avoiding these foods, the gut quickly improves. Those who are sensitive to high-FODMAP foods often experience bloating and IBS symptoms. Low-FODMAP foods can be integrated into other wellness diets. Visit my blog to read more about the Low-FODMAP diet. Type "Low-FODMAP food lists" into the search engine at EatBeautiful.net to see which foods to eat and which foods to avoid. Use these lists to substitute ingredients in soup and stew recipes. You may need to avoid foods like onions, garlic and winter squash, but Low-FODMAP foods like zucchini, parsnips, potatoes or sweet potatoes will sub in well. Please feel free to email me if you have a substitution question for one of the recipes in this cookbook.

LOW-HISTAMINE

For those struggling with Mast Cell Activation Syndrome or a histamine overload, often manifested by allergies, rashes or hives, it may be necessary to temporarily reduce histamine intake. High-histamine foods are usually aged. Foods that are not high in histamines themselves but that encourage mast cells to release histamines should also be avoided, as they may cause the same symptoms. Often, these foods may be added back into one's diet after a period of regaining balance or healing leaky gut. When using this cookbook, opt for meat stocks instead of bone broths.

Use fresh meat, and avoid leftovers. Read more about how I recovered from histamine over-reactivity on my blog. Type "histamine recovery tips" into the search engine at EatBeautiful.net.

LECTIN-FREE

Lectins are proteins often found in foods containing seeds, with some exceptions. Lectins are also found in some roots and in early-stage leaves. Plants use lectins as defensive mechanisms for their survival. When humans eat foods containing lectins, the lectins may actually cause leaky gut or be antagonistic to the gut lining. Personally, I have found this theory to be true. I have given up many foods that contain lectins, and found better gut health as a result.

For information about low-histamine and lectin-free diets, visit EAT BEAUTIFUL *(www.eatbeautiful.net); search "low-histamine" and "lectin-free."*

INDEX

PALEO *Soups and Stews*

GAPS *Soups and Stews*

GAPS INTRO Soups and Stews

Hamburger Soup | *14*
Chicken Zoodle Soup | *16*
Thanksgiving Soup | *18*
Fresh Sole or Flounder With Celery Root and Artichokes | *20*
Turkey Sage Soup | *22*
White Carrot Ginger Soup | *24*
Savoy Cabbage and Lemongrass Soup, With Chicken, Mushrooms and Garlic | *41*
Pho With Vegetable Noodles and Beef Short Ribs (GAPS Intro+) | *43*
Easy Cold Yogurt Cucumber Soup | *127*

A I P *Soups and Stews*

Basic Chicken Meatballs Soup | *2*
Bone Marrow Soup | *3*
Cilantro Bisque Twin Soups With Seafood Meatballs (or Pork Meatballs) | *7*
15-Minute Beef Stew With Skirt Steak | *9*
Fall and Winter Meatball Soup | *11*
Simple Fennel and Cauliflower Rice Soup With Shredded Chicken | *12*
Hamburger Soup | *14*
Chicken Zoodle Soup | *16*
Thanksgiving Soup | *18*
Fresh Sole or Flounder With Celery Root and Artichokes | *20*
Turkey Sage Soup | *22*
White Carrot Ginger Soup | *24*
Beef Short Ribs With White Peach and Apple Chutney | *25*
Savory Breakfast Mash Stew With Sausages or Grass-fed Hot Dogs | *27*
Beef Tenderloin Skewers With Pineapple Stew | *32*
Thai Salmon Soup (Tom Kha Gai) | *34*
French Cabbage Soup With Bacon and Sausage (AIP+) | *36*
Beef Stew With White Sweet Potatoes and Carrots | *39*
Savoy Cabbage and Lemongrass Soup, With Chicken, Mushrooms and Garlic | *41*
Pho With Vegetable Noodles and Beef Short Ribs (AIP+) | *43*
Hearty Nomato Beef Minestrone | *45*
Vietnamese Shrimp Soup | *47*
Clams and Garlic in Broth (AIP+) | *49*
Eggroll in a Bowl Soup | *51*

Sweet Breakfast Mash Stew With Berries and Ginger | 52
Cream of Cauliflower and Parsnip Soup | 54
Trotters, Neck or Beef Tail Curry (AIP+) | 56
Parsnip and Mushroom Soup With Pork and Bacon | 58
Chicken Pot Pie Baked Stew | 60
Spiced Lamb Stew With Sweet Potatoes (AIP+) | 64
Healthy Chocolate Soup (AIP+) | 65
Chicken and Apple Soup With Paprika, Sage and Chives (AIP+) | 68
Japanese Udon Soup (AIP+) | 74
Winter Squash Stew With Chinese Five-Spice, Pork and Kale (AIP+) | 83
Borscht (AIP+) | 118
Extra-Creamy Cream of Pumpkin Soup With Bacon Garnish (AIP+) | 119
Thai Chard Bisque (AIP+) | 121

K E T O *Soups and Stews*

Basic Chicken Meatballs Soup | 2
15-Minute Beef Stew With Skirt Steak | 9
Simple Fennel and Cauliflower Rice Soup With Shredded Chicken | 12
Hamburger Soup | 14
Chicken Zoodle Soup | 16
Fresh Sole or Flounder With Celery Root and Artichokes | 20
Savory Breakfast Mash Stew With Sausages or Grass-fed Hot Dogs | 27
Thai Salmon Soup (Tom Kha Gai) | 34
French Cabbage Soup With Bacon and Sausage | 36
Savoy Cabbage and Lemongrass Soup, With Chicken, Mushrooms and Garlic | 41
Pho With Vegetable Noodles and Beef Short Ribs | 43
Clams and Garlic in Broth | 49
Eggroll in a Bowl Soup | 51
Trotters, Neck or Beef Tail Curry | 56
Healthy Chocolate Soup | 65
Israeli Ground Lamb Stew With Lemon and Tahini | 72
Japanese Udon Soup | 74
Indian Lamb Curry | 76
Italian Stuffed Pepper Soup | 78
Shrimp Ceviche (Chilled) | 80

Miso Soup | 89
Hearty Chili With Mushrooms and Red Bell Peppers | 97
Chinese Sesame Chicken | 99
Gumbo | 101
Easy Cabbage Roll Soup | 103
Broccoli White Cheddar Soup | 106
Broccoli and Cheddar Buffalo Chicken Soup | 108
Chicken and Aged Cheddar Cauliflower Soup | 110
Chicken Cordon Bleu Stew | 112
Butter Chicken | 114
Cheeseburger Soup | 116
Thai Chard Bisque | 121
Indian Spinach Stew With Cheese Cubes (Palaak Paneer Variation) | 123
Smoky Enchilada Stew | 125
Easy Cold Yogurt Cucumber Soup | 127

VAD Soups and Stews

Basic Chicken Meatballs Soup | 2
Bone Marrow Soup | 3
15-Minute Beef Stew With Skirt Steak | 9
Fall and Winter Meatball Soup (VAD+) | 11
Simple Fennel and Cauliflower Rice Soup With Shredded Chicken | 12
Hamburger Soup (VAD+) | 14
Chicken Zoodle Soup (VAD+) | 16
Fresh Sole or Flounder With Celery Root and Artichokes | 20
White Carrot Ginger Soup | 24
Beef Short Ribs With White Peach and Apple Chutney | 25
Savory Breakfast Mash Stew With Sausages or Grass-fed Hot Dogs | 27
Apple Soup | 29
Beef Tenderloin Skewers With Pineapple Stew | 32
French Cabbage Soup With Turkey Sausage (VAD+) | 36
Beef Stew With White Sweet Potatoes and Carrots (VAD+) | 39
Pho With Vegetable Noodles and Beef Short Ribs (VAD+) | 43
Cream of Cauliflower and Parsnip Soup | 54
Trotters, Neck or Beef Tail Curry | 56

Healthy Chocolate Soup | 65
Yellow Split Pea Soup | 70
Pumpkin or Parsnip-Tahini Bisque With Turmeric, Ginger and Onions | 93
Golden Macadamia Stew With Chicken Satay Skewers | 95
Chinese Sesame Chicken | 99

INSTANT POT *Soups and Stews*

Simple Fennel and Cauliflower Rice Soup With Shredded Chicken | 12
Chicken Zoodle Soup | 16
Turkey Sage Soup | 22
Beef Short Ribs With White Peach and Apple Chutney | 25
Savory Breakfast Mash Stew With Sausages or Grass-fed Hot Dogs | 27
Beef Stew With White Sweet Potatoes and Carrots | 39
Pho With Vegetable Noodles and Beef Short Ribs | 43
Vietnamese Shrimp Soup | 47
Sweet Breakfast Mash Stew With Berries and Ginger | 52
Cream of Cauliflower and Parsnip Soup | 54
Trotters, Neck or Beef Tail Curry | 56
Spiced Lamb Stew With Sweet Potatoes | 64
Yellow Split Pea Soup | 70
Indian Lamb Curry | 76
Italian Stuffed Pepper Soup | 78
Sprouted Lentil and Ham Hock Soup With Onions, Apples and Fennel | 87
Mexican Pork and Green Bean Stew | 90
Hearty Chili With Mushrooms and Red Bell Peppers | 97
Chinese Sesame Chicken | 99
Broccoli and Cheddar Buffalo Chicken Soup | 108
Butter Chicken | 114
Borscht | 118

"DUMP AND COOK" *Soups and Stews*

Chicken Zoodle Soup | *16*
Pho With Vegetable Noodles and Beef Short Ribs | *43*
Vietnamese Shrimp Soup | *47*
Cream of Cauliflower and Parsnip Soup | *54*
Trotters, Neck or Beef Tail Curry | *56*
Spiced Lamb Stew With Sweet Potatoes | *64*
Hearty Chili With Mushrooms and Red Bell Peppers | *97*
Butter Chicken | *114*

SPECIAL THANKS

to the following people and animals:

Tim Stevens — You the best.

Kids — You the best, too.

Goldie — We're waiting for you. Thanks for being in my heart, all through the writing of this book.

Kitties — You often got in my way when I was trying to type, but you more than made up for it with all the love. I am so grateful for the joy you bring.

Avi — You make my doorstep such a happy place.

Mom — Thank you for every Wednesday, every gift of groceries or other, every walk. I appreciate you!

Daddle — Man, you're still a rock to me.

Jilly — You always support me in the most needed of times. #thankful for our bond.

Wardeh Harmon — As always, the dearest of friends and the best of mentors.

Sonya Hemmings — The best editor and such a lovely person, I am privileged to have you on my team again — this time as designer, too! Thank you.

Charlotte Dupont — I only thought of one person to take the photos of me, and that is you. Unique and giving, I so appreciate your gift with people and photography.

And for all these blessings, I thank my great God.

Made in the USA
Las Vegas, NV
13 December 2023

82768220R00112